Parentice

JOHN F.

KENNEDY

Parentie

JOHN F.
KENNEDY:

THE MAN, THE POLITICIAN,
THE PRESIDENT

Edited by Thomas C. Reeves
The University of Wisconsin—Parkside

ROBERT E. KRIEGER PUBLISHING COMPANY
MALABAR, FLORIDA
1990

Original Edition 1990

Printed and Published by
ROBERT E. KRIEGER PUBLISHING CO., INC.
KRIEGER DRIVE
MALABAR, FLORIDA 32950

Copyright © 1990 by Robert E. Krieger Publishing Co., Inc.

Library of Congress Cataloging-in-Publication Data

John F. Kennedy : the man, the politician, the president / edited by
 Thomas C. Reeves.
  p. cm.
 Bibliography: p.
 ISBN 0-89464-371-1 (pbk.)
  1. Kennedy John F. (John Fitzgerald), 1917–1963. 2. Presidents—
United States—Biography. 3. United States—Politics and
government—1961–1963. 4. United States—Politics and
government—1953–1961. I. Reeves. Thomas C., 1936–
E842.J638 1990
973.922′092—dc20
[B]   89-33503
                                                                 CIP

10 9 8 7 6 5 4 3 2

Contents

Introduction   vii

Part One   **The Man**   1

1. *James MacGregor Burns*   Young Kennedy   3
2. *Arthur M. Schlesinger, Jr.*   The Student, the War Hero, the Writer   12
3. *Joan and Clay Blair, Jr.*   The Kennedys in Another Light   17
4. *Theodore C. Sorensen*   Mind and Character   24
5. *Herbert S. Parmet*   The Congressman, the Author   28

Part Two   **The Campaigner**   35

6. *Kenneth P. O'Donnell*
and David F. Powers   The First Campaign   37
7. *Richard J. Whalen*   The First Senate Race   43
8. *Theodore H. White*   The Presidential Contest   53
9. *Richard Goodwin*   On The Inside in 1960   61

Part Three   **The Communicator**   69

10. *The Inaugural Address*   71
11. *Pierre Salinger*   The President and the Mass Media   75
12. *Benjamin Bradlee*   The Manipulator   81

Part Four   **The Domestic Scene**   87

13. *Gary Wills*   Kennedy's Eggheads   89
14. *David Burner*   The Domestic Programs   95
15. *Bruce Miroff*   Prosperity and the New Frontier   99
16. *Carl M. Brauer*   The Issue of Race   104

Part Five	**Foreign Policy**	109
17. *David Burner and Thomas R. West*	Cold War Liberalism	111
18. *Peter Collier and David Horowitz*	Reckless and Ruthless	118
19. *I. F. Stone*	The Missile Crisis	123
20. *Herbert S. Parmet*	Vietnam	130
21. *The American University Speech*		137
Part Six	**The Legacy**	145
22. *Thomas G. Paterson*	An Ardent Cold Warrior	147
23. *Midge Decter*	The Unprincipled	149
24. *David E. Kaiser*	The Incarnation of an Era	152
25. *William E. Leuchtenburg*	Kennedy As Myth	156
	Suggestions for Further Reading	161

Introduction

Few American politicians have ever been so widely revered as John F. Kennedy. During his presidency, Kennedy made consistently high scores in the Gallup polls, reaching a high of 83 percent after the Bay of Pigs and staying within the 60th and 70th percentile until the fall of 1963. Many journalists and intellectuals fawned over him, convinced that he had brought a new sense of style, vigor, and purpose to the White House. Many blacks cheered his efforts to improve race relations. Millions applauded his determination to stand up to the Communists. Hardly anyone could fail to admire the handsome young President's televised interviews, speeches, and press conferences.

The assassination in 1963 prompted expressions of grief from all over the world. Journalists were soon calling Kennedy "the pride of western civilization" and "a bright, racing star who lighted men's thoughts and their dreams." Historian Arthur

Schlesinger, Jr., who served as a Special Assistant to the President, exclaimed: "He re-established the republic as the first generation of our leaders saw it—young, brave, civilized, rational, gay, tough, questing, exultant in the excitement and potentiality of history. He transformed the American spirit. . . ."

Since that time, Americans have continued to admire Kennedy. A poll published in 1983 by *Newsweek* showed him to be the nation's most popular President. Worshipful tributes occurred in 1983 and 1988 when Americans commemorated the assassination. Michael Dukakis, the Democratic Presidential candidate in 1988, repeatedly declared his fondness for Kennedy and imitated some of the late President's oratorical phrases and mannerisms. Each year hundreds of thousands visit the assassination site in Dallas, the grave at Arlington Cemetery, and the Kennedy Library, near Boston.

For about a decade after Kennedy's death, the Camelot image of the New Frontier was virtually unchallenged. Scores of books and articles by Kennedy relatives, friends, and employees heaped praise upon the fallen hero. Arthur Schlesinger, Jr.'s *A Thousand Days: John F. Kennedy In The White House* and Theodore C. Sorensen's *Kennedy* were sophisticated and highly-praised monuments that few thought assailable. Kennedy secretary Evelyn Lincoln dedicated *My Twelve Years With John F. Kennedy* "With Love To Caroline and John," the late President's children, and that sort of sentiment was common in the literature of the mid-1960s and early 1970s. An assortment of television programs echoed the cheers, showing a Chief Executive who was good-looking, articulate, witty, and well informed. After Lyndon Johnson, Richard Nixon, and Gerald Ford, many looked wistfully at the Thousand Days.

Some attitudes began to change, however, as America became more deeply embroiled in Vietnam. Several left-wing scholars and journalists, such as Richard Walton and Bruce Miroff, traced the war to JFK and his advisers and portrayed Camelot as the home of extreme cold warriors and lackeys of corporate wealth. *The Pentagon Papers*, published in 1971, provided interesting evidence.

In 1975, the standard view of Kennedy and his Administration was seriously shaken. A Senate committee revealed evidence of Kennedy's often shocking use of the Central Intelligence Agency in Cuba and Southeast Asia. Moreover, a leak from a staff member led to the disclosure of a Kennedy mistress, Judith Campbell Exner. While secretly visiting the White House on numerous occasions, Exner was also intimately involved with two top Mafia figures employed by the CIA to assassinate Cuban Premier Fidel Castro. Additional evidence soon appeared about Kennedy's life-long pursuit of young women. One target of his attentions exclaimed, "I know he had a lot of girlfriends. God Almighty, he used to pick them up off the street."

That same year, liberal journalist Benjamin C. Bradlee, a close friend of the late President and his wife, published *Conversations With Kennedy*. The JFK revealed in its pages barely resembled the almost sacred figure enshrined in earlier literature. The President was exceedingly vain, perpetually foul-mouthed, petty, penurious, insensitive, spiteful, eager for salacious gossip, manipulative, and not nearly as brilliant as others had claimed (Kennedy's I.Q. was 119). The memoirs of *Chicago Tribune* newsman Walter Trohan and Washington reporter Nancy Hanschman Dickerson contained more evidence damaging to Kennedy's reputation.

Objective scholarship entered the picture in 1976. *The Search For J.F.K.* by Joan and Clay Blair, Jr. was a superb study based on thousands of newly-released documents and more than 150 oral interviews. Focussing their attention upon Kennedy's life to 1947, the Blairs corrected numerous cover-ups and fabrications about Kennedy's physical health, education, and war record. They proved, for example, that Jack had been extremely sickly all of his life, and in 1947 was diagnosed as having Addison's Disease. After carefully reconstructing Kennedy's famous PT-109 exploits, the authors concluded, "He was, in effect, a 'manufactured' war hero." The Blairs also added new dimensions to our understanding of Kennedy's character, revealing emotional problems stemming in part from difficulties with his imperious, demanding, and lecherous father.

Other scholars and journalists soon contributed more information and insight. In 1980, historian Herbert S. Parmet published *Jack, The Struggles Of John F. Kennedy*, a reliable account based on extensive research. Three years later, Parmet brought out *JFK: The Presidency Of John F. Kennedy*, again receiving favorable reviews. In 1984, *The Kennedys, An American Drama*, by Peter Collier and David Horowitz, and *The Kennedys: Dynasty And Disaster*, by John H. Davis, expanded our knowledge of the Kennedys and further documented the darker side of JFK's character.

Kennedy's partisans responded with numerous articles and books. Arthur Schlesinger Jr.'s *Robert Kennedy And His Times* and Doris Kearns Goodwin's *The Fitzgeralds And The Kennedys* were the most impressive replies to revisionist accounts. Judging from opinion polls and the media events marking the President's assassination, the traditional view of Kennedy and Camelot remains firmly entrenched in the public mind. In July 1988, the popular Sunday newspaper magazine *Parade* contained a worshipful article entitled "Our Brother, John Fitzgerald Kennedy," by Senator Edward Kennedy. "In the brief time Jack had, he touched our hearts with fire, and the glow from that fire still lights the world." That year, publishers brought out more than two dozen volumes, most of them brimming over with veneration. Scores of often gushy tributes appeared on television.

Scholars, however, tend to be divided about Kennedy and his Administration. Even well-established college textbooks offer conflicting views. A poll of 75 prominent historians and journalists published by *American Heritage* in 1988 ranked Kennedy the most overrated public figure in American history. On the other hand, historian David Burner's impressive *John F. Kennedy And A New Generation*, appearing about the same time, remained positive. Meanwhile, memoirs and specialized studies continue to appear with regularity, offering a variety of judgments about Kennedy the man, the politician, and the President.

This volume presents a sampling of the controversy in the hope that readers will not only grasp a measure of the literature but will also be stimulated to delve further into one of the most provocative and fascinating subjects in recent American history.

James MacGregor Burns describes Jack's parents and life in the Kennedy family. What was the family attitude toward "Yankee blue bloods"? How important was Joseph P. Kennedy's stress on competition? Does it seem likely that the elder Kennedy did not "force his views" on his children? What overall impression of Jack Kennedy does Burns present?

Arthur Schlesinger, Jr. discusses Kennedy's life at Harvard, his first book, his military service, and his brief career as a journalist. What were Kennedy's "preoccupations" with courage and death? What were his thoughts about the United Nations? Why was he pessimistic about the future of the United States?

Joan and Clay Blair, Jr. reevaluate much of Jack's early life and reexamine his wartime experiences. How valuable are the observations of Betty Spalding? Why does so much misleading information about Jack's health and intellect appear in standard biographies? How much of Kennedy's PT-109 activity should be described as heroic?

Kennedy's most important employee and confidant, Theodore C. Sorensen, describes Jack's character, personality, and intellect. What were some of the "increasingly deep convictions" Sorensen noted? Was Kennedy's sense of tragedy useful? How much of a liberal was Kennedy?

Herbert S. Parmet examines the question of Addison's Disease and its relationship to Kennedy's activities while in Congress. How did the illness affect Jack's over-all attitude? In this selection, does Kennedy appear to be "full of ideals"? Why was it important for Jack to be perceived as an author?

Kenneth P. O'Donnell and David F. Powers recount the campaign of 1946. Why was Powers so deeply attracted to the young candidate? Why did so many women "go crazy over him"? How could Kennedy have had an "incredible stamina and zest for hard work" if in fact he was as ill as the Blairs and Parmet described him?

Richard J. Whalen describes the importance of Joseph P. Kennedy to the Senate race of 1952. Why was the elder Kennedy so eager to defeat Lodge? How significant were money and publicity in the campaign? What was the leading campaign issue? What role did Senator Joe McCarthy play? In what ways were all of the Kennedy family members helpful?

Theodore H. White recalls his experiences with Kennedy during the presidential campaign of 1960. Why did the candidate telephone Martin Luther King? Why were Kennedy crowds "frenzied"? Why did reporters overwhelmingly favor Kennedy over Nixon?

Kennedy speechwriter Richard Goodwin recalls several events during the 1960 campaign that shed light on the candidate. Why did Kennedy and his people despise Nixon? What was the candidate's approach toward religion? Why did Kennedy "win" the first television debate?

The President's Inaugural Address, at least in large part a product of Sorensen's talented pen, thrilled millions at the time and continues to be cited as one of Kennedy's most effective speeches. What does it reveal about the new Chief Executive's vision of the future? Why the strong emphasis on foreign affairs and military preparedness in a time of peace?

Kennedy press secretary Pierre Salinger discusses the President's skillful use of the mass media and his friendly relations with reporters. Note especially the special favors given to major columnists. How effective were Kennedy's efforts in creating and sustaining a positive public image?

Liberal journalist Benjamin Bradlee, a personal friend of the Kennedys, describes how the President used him to obtain favorable press coverage. Is there more than a little Presidential cynicism revealed here? And recklessness? What does Kennedy's crude language reveal about him?

Gary Wills is interested in the cultural advances allegedly generated by Kennedy and his advisers. How much of a renaissance actually began in Washington under Kennedy? What does it mean to say, "Camelot was the opium of the intellectuals"? Was Kennedy merely manipulating "the best and the brightest"?

Historian David Burner ruminates on the New Frontier's domestic policy and the President's relationship with Congress. Why were the Admnistration's achievements at home so minimal? Why did Kennedy "put domestic issues aside whenever he could"?

Bruce Miroff gives the Administration credit for increasing national prosperity, but he condemns the gap between rich and poor. What was Kennedy's "Keynesian Revolution" designed to achieve? Was the president in fact an economic conservative? Why would the President attempt to increase the wealth of those who mostly opposed him?

Carl M. Brauer describes Kennedy's attitude toward civil rights and summarizes the Administration's efforts in the field. If Kennedy was "a consummate politician," why would he alienate the powerful Southern wing of his party by pushing for racial equality? Do Administration achievements in civil rights prove that Kennedy was a man of strong moral convictions?

David Burner and Thomas R. West explore the Administration's overall view of foreign affairs and discuss the Bay of Pigs and the Alliance for Progress. What was "sophisticated" anti-Communism? What was "the technocrat liberal mind"? Why were some Kennedy advisers unable to "get through" to the President?

Peter Collier and David Horowitz point to the darker side of the Kennedys' approach to Cuba. How important was the Attorney General in making foreign policy? How likely is it that the Kennedy brothers were aware of the assassination efforts against Fidel Castro? In 1988, Judith Campbell Exner, dying of cancer, admitted that for eighteen months in 1960 and 1961 she carried envelopes back and forth between Kennedy and Sam Giancana. She also arranged about ten secret meetings between the two men. Does this new information alter our view of JFK in any meaningful way?

I. F. Stone credits Soviet Premier Khrushchev with ending a conflict that threatened the lives of hundreds of millions throughout the world. The author is appalled by the Kennedy brothers, thinking them immature, dangerous, and politically motivated. We now know that Bobby quietly offered to exchange American missiles in Turkey for Soviet missiles in Cuba, and that the subsequent deal apparently settled the crisis. Does this fact greatly affect Stone's argument?

Herbert S. Parmet describes Administration policy toward Vietnam. Why did Kennedy "waver" about efforts to bring down Diem? Why did he think it necessary to send a secret ambassador to South Vietnam?

The President's mid-1963 American University speech has been called a breakthrough in Cold War rhetoric and a definitive answer to those who see Kennedy as a rigid anti-Communist. What kind of peace did Kennedy seek? What exactly was he prepared to do to rid the world of war? To what extent, in his judgment, were the Soviets evil?

The evaluations by Thomas G. Paterson, Midge Decter, David E. Kaiser, and William E. Leuchtenburg vary, of course, and should be studied with care. Which interpretation best seems to fit the evidence? Which appears to be the most objective? It is not as important to come away from this book with the "right" view as it is to have an understanding of the complexity of history and to have a strong desire to learn more about the life and times of John F. Kennedy.

Part One THE MAN

Chapter 1 YOUNG KENNEDY

JAMES MACGREGOR BURNS (b. 1918) has
been a political scientist at Williams College
since 1941. Selected to be JFK's first biogra-
pher, Burns remains a great admirer of the
Kennedy family. Among his numerous books
is *Edward Kennedy And The Camelot Legacy*.
In this selection, what people seem especially
important in the moulding of young John F.
Kennedy?

Some East Bostonians raised their eyebrows when they heard that Pat's eldest boy,
Joseph Patrick Kennedy, had won the hand of Rose Fitzgerald, the mayor's daughter,
one of the most eligible Catholic girls in town. This was pretty good for the son of a
ward boss and saloonkeeper. But those who knew Joe Kennedy were not surprised. He
was a go-getter in everything he tried, they said, and he would be a good husband and
a good provider.

They were right. Only nine years after his birth in 1888, Joe had sold peanuts and
candy on Boston excursion boats, and a few years later had worked as office boy in a
bank. He attended parochial school until seventh grade, then shifted to Boston Latin,
the famed school where Benjamin Franklin and Henry Adams had been students. This

From *John Kennedy, a Political Profile* by James MacGregor Burns, copyright 1961. Reprinted by
permission of Harcourt Brace Jovanovich, Inc.

meant getting up early to catch the North Ferry every morning, at a penny a trip, but it was worth it, for at Boston Latin Joe mixed with youths from elite Back Bay and the West End and not just East Boston. He was a popular boy and a fine athlete. His favorite sport was baseball, which he played so well that he won the mayor's cup, presented by his future father-in-law, the great John F. himself.

His mother, ambitious for her son, wanted Joe to go to Harvard, and he entered with the class of 1912. He made the baseball team his junior year. His popularity and athletic prowess helped him get elected to the undergraduate societies Dicky, Delta Upsilon, and Hasty Pudding, but he never made the so-called best clubs. His grades were only mediocre; once when the baseball captain warned him that he was dangerously low in an economics course, he switched to music. But he revered some of the great teachers at Harvard—men like Bliss Perry and Charles Copeland—and he felt flattered when "Copey" dropped by his room and invited him to his famous readings.

Looking at the American scene through his calm, appraising eyes, Joe could see that sports and politics and literature were fun, but money really talked. During the summer vacations he and a partner earned several thousand dollars by running a sightseeing bus to historic Lexington. He vowed to make a million by the time he was thirty-five, and he did, probably several times over. After he graduated from Harvard in 1912, he got a job as a bank examiner and learned the practical side of finance. When a small East Boston bank, owned in part by members of his family, was about to be taken over by another bank, Joe rounded up some capital and proxies and, with the help of his family, was elected bank president at the age of twenty-five, reportedly the youngest in the country.

By then he was courting Rose Fitzgerald, and the two were married in the private chapel of Cardinal O'Connell in Boston in October 1914. With her dark hair and rosy cheeks, the bride had her father's good looks and charm, but she also showed something of her mother's dignity and serenity. She had gone to parochial and public school and studied music in Europe; she was popular and a good student. The couple settled down in a $6,500 house in a respectable, lower-middle-class neighborhood in Brookline. The groom, in debt at the time as a result of buying the bank stock, had to borrow money to make the down payment. But he was soon solvent. Children came rapidly: the first, Joe, Jr., within a year of the marriage, followed by another boy, John F., in 1917, then five girls and a son—Rosemary, Kathleen, Eunice, Patricia, Jean, and Robert F.—during the 1920's, and finally another son, Edward, in 1932.

With the coming of World War I in 1917, Kennedy resigned from the bank and became assistant general manager of Bethelehem Steel's huge shipyards in Quincy. After the war he moved swiftly toward his first million. Boston finance was still controlled by conservative Yankees not very sympathetic to aggressive Irishmen, but Kennedy, acting on the old political maxim, "If you can't lick 'em, join 'em," deliberately studied the habits of Boston financiers, even to the point of taking a seat near them on the train. One of these, Galen Stone, was so impressed that he hired him as head of his investment banking house, Hayden, Stone and Company, and in this job

Kennedy learned market operations and began to speculate on his own. He took some hard losses, recouped them, and then, with a group of Bostonians, bought control of a chain of thirty-one small movie theaters scattered throughout New England.

But many a Yankee banker still could not wholly accept Joe Kennedy. It was all right for Irishmen to run little East Boston banks and handle immigrants' remittances, they felt, but not to crash the central citadels of finance. So Kennedy, disgusted, began to operate more and more in New York and Hollywood. During the mid-1920's, he moved in on the booming turbulent movie industry, won control of several motion-picture companies, re-shuffled them, and sold out at a huge profit. Independently, he produced two features starring Gloria Swanson, who had become a close family friend, but one was so vivid, involving a seduction scene of a convent girl, that he refused to exhibit it.

By this time Kennedy was a business legend and a man of mystery. Long after he quit the movies in the late '20s, people were arguing about whether he had left behind him a string of strengthened companies or heaps of wreckage. When he deserted Hollywood and began to speculate in the bull market, his operations became even more obscure. "He moved in the intense, secretive circles of operators in the wildest stock market in history," *Fortune* later commented, "with routine plots and pools, inside information and wild guesses. . . ." But Kennedy came out of the bull market with many millions, made more in the crash, and even more by shrewd speculation in liquor importing, real estate, and numerous other enterprises joined together in a financial labyrinth that probably only the financier himself understood. . . . Kennedy had been raised in a heavily political atmosphere; he says today that one of his first memories was of two men coming to his father and reporting in a matter-of-fact way, "Pat, we voted 128 times today." But Boston politics, with its petty intrigues and backbiting, bored him. Having made his millions, he moved up through politics, as Pat and Honey Fitz had done, but on a national scale. In 1932 he supported Roosevelt before the convention and gave $15,000 to the Democratic campaign fund, lent it $50,000 more, and probably contributed many more thousands indirectly. In 1934 the President made him first head of the new Securities and Exchange Commission—to the consternation of some—and later, head of the Maritime Commission. Two years later, in 1936, Kennedy wrote a ringing endorsement of the Democratic nominee in a book called *I'm for Roosevelt*, and he gave the Democrats another big campaign donation. . . .

Joe Kennedy's great consolation in these strenuous years was his family. Indeed, he justified his feverish money-making largely as a way of ensuring his nine children's security in the years to come. Explaining to visitors why he could go on despite suspicion and criticism, he liked to quote a senator's reply to an angry voter who threatened to drive him out of office: "Home holds no terrors for me.". . . .

Even among his family, however, Kennedy could not escape from the press of finance and politics; perhaps he did not try. At home he was pursued by telegrams and long-distance calls, and the house was full of aides, politicians, financiers. Visitors would find him happily stretched out on the big porch at Hyannisport, a stock-market ticker chattering away at his side.

Actually, Kennedy had no wish to seal his children off from the outside world. They might as well know at the start that it was harshly competitive. "Every single kid," a close friend of the family told a reporter, "was raised to think, First, what shall I do about this problem? Second, what will Dad say about my solution of it?" When he was home he encouraged talk at the dinner table about American government and politics, but money matters could not be raised. "I have never discussed money with my wife and family," Kennedy said years later, "and I never will."

The father wanted his children to be competitive with one another, and they vied among themselves fiercely in parlor games and sports. Sometimes the girls would leave the tennis courts sobbing after being bested by their brothers. Touch football games were almost fratricidal. "They are the most competitive and at the same time the most cohesive family I've ever seen," said another long-time family friend some years after. "They fight each other, yet they feed on each other. They stimulate each other. Their minds strike sparks. Each of them has warm friends. But none they like and admire so much as they like and admire their own brothers and sisters."

He wanted his children, however competitive they might be with one another, to present a united front against the outside world. Consciously or not, he was copying the ways of his father and the Democratic bosses of old, who allowed fighting among the district leaders between elections but not on the day when they had to beat Republicans. The fierce loyalty of the Kennedys to each other exists to this day and has been especially helpful to John Kennedy in his political campaigns.

During Kennedy's long absences, Joe, Jr. increasingly assumed his father's family responsibilities. He taught the others how to sail and swim with something of Joe, Sr.'s perfectionism. Indeed, he was much like his father—generous, considerate, and loving, and, at the same time, driving domineering, and hot-tempered.

But the main steadying element in this boisterous household was Rose Kennedy. Even as a young woman, she impressed her friends with her scrupulous sense of duty and her devotion to the church. What she lacked in intellectual brilliance she made up in her intense love for her family. Love and a sense of duty were needed in the Kennedy home. The children were so numerous that she had to keep records of their vaccinations, illnesses, food problems, and the like, on file cards, but she was still able to give each child some individual attention. Somehow she survived and even thrived, keeping her face unlined and her figure as modish as ever. Years later, on meeting this mother of nine still looking so young, a gallant gentleman took her hand and exclaimed, "At last—I believe in the stork!"

In her husband's absence, she would even work up current-events topics and guide the discussion of them by the children at the table—her husband would have expected it. With him away so often and for so long, the daily routine, despite household help, was not simple, certainly not so easy as it later seemed to some of the family. Occasionally—and more often as the children went off to school—she got out from under her big family by taking vacations with her husband in Florida or Europe. She also devoted herself increasingly to the church. "She was terribly religious," Kennedy says. "She was a little removed, and still is, which I think is the only way to survive when you have nine children. I thought she was a very model mother for a big family.". . . .

John Fitzgerald Kennedy was born on May 29, 1917, in Brookline, a suburb of Boston. America had just entered the war, and about this time his father left to take his post at the Fore River shipyards. For several years the family lived at 83 Beals Street, in a large frame house set back a bit from the sidewalk on a small plot. It was a quiet, lower-middle-class area, the other side of town from East Boston. Here Jack spent his early childhood—years that he hardly remembers today.

As his father became more prosperous, the family moved to higher-class houses and neighborhoods, pursuing the Yankee blue bloods, who still outdistanced them in social prestige. The next stop on the way was on the corner of Naples and Abbotsford Roads in Brookline, in a bigger house with a dozen rooms for the rapidly growing Kennedy family. Here Jack and his older brother, Joe, romped on the long porch that stretched halfway around the house, read picture books in front of the fireplaces in the old-fashioned, high-ceilinged living room and parlor, raced each other under the shade trees outside. Here, too, Jack first went to grade school. Dexter School, about six blocks from the Kennedy home, was a private academy, but not a parochial school; Joe and Jack may have been at the time its only Catholic students.

Sometimes Grandpa Fitz, still a booster of Boston, would pick the boys up and take them to a Red Sox game or to the swan boats in Boston's Public Garden or to some other favorite haunt. One of Jack's earliest memories is of touring the wards with his grandfather when Fitz was running for governor in 1922. Fitz even tried out some of his speeches with the six-year-old boy as an audience of one. Rose took the older children on historical pilgrimages—to the Yankee landmarks of Plymouth Rock, Concord Bridge, and Bunker Hill—strengthening their allegiance to the family's adopted land. Sundays the family drove over to spend the afternoon with old Pat Kennedy, who was now in his sixties and less active in politics. To the children, Grandfather Kennedy was a kind but somewhat awesome figure. "On those Sunday afternoon visits he wouldn't let us cut up or even wink in his presence," Kennedy recalls.

But the pleasant Boston days were soon over. Joseph Kennedy had outgrown his native city, and he settled his family near the center of his New York financial empire, first in Riverdale and then in Bronxville. The Bronxville house has since been torn down and the lot subdivided, but it was a rather affluent place surrounded by broad lawns where the children played baseball and football. Jack went to fourth, fifth, and sixth grades at nearby Riverdale School; the teachers remembered him later as a rather slight boy, polite, industrious, and likable, with a special interest in English history— and a hot temper. His mother came to school often to check solicitously on her son's progress; his father sometimes invited the teachers to the house to see private showings of the latest movies.

Looking back today, Kennedy cannot remember any unhappy times during his childhood. It was an easy, prosperous life, supervised by maids and nurses, with more and more younger sisters to boss and to play with. . . .

At thirteen, Jack left his Bronxville home for boarding school. For a year he went to Canterbury School in New Milford, Connecticut, the only Catholic school he ever attended. After an initial bout with homesickness—"I felt pretty homesick but it's O.K. now"—he settled easily into the life of the school. . . .

Always a ready competitor, he tried out for football, baseball, and other sports, with fair success. He reported that he could swim fifth yards in thirty seconds; this swimming skill would save his life many years later. . . .

The next fall he shifted to Choate, a rather select private school with a strong Episcopal flavor, in Wallinford, Connecticut, where Adlai Stevenson and Chester Bowles had been students years before. Joe, Jr. was there, making out well. The boys' father chose Choate because he wanted them to mix and compete with a greater variety of boys than in a Catholic school. . . . As at Canterbury, he went out for a half-dozen sports, but failed to make the varsity. Coaches found him an eager, scrappy player in intramural games yet reluctant to apply himself in practice. In his studies his Latin was still low, his French not much better, his English and history only fair. To some teachers he seemed content to coast along as a "gentleman C scholar." He graduated sixty-fourth in a class of 112. But to his classmates, if not to his teachers, he must have shown some glimpse of his potential ability and later drive, for they voted him "the most likely to succeed."

As his father's riches piled up in the 1920's, Jack spent many winter vacations at the family's new resort home at Palm Beach and summers at another home at Hyannisport, on Cape Cod. He especially loved Hyannisport, and still does. The big house there looked out over a long beach, a tennis court, and a well-tended lawn handy for softball and other family games. Jutting out from the beach was a breakwater shielding the yachts of the summer fold. Jack's competitive instinct showed up early—he named his first sailboat "Victura," which he explained was Latin "meaning something about winning."

But life was not always a victory. Wherever he was, as school or at home, Jack was conscious of his father's incessant concern that he do better, especially in his studies. His letters home were full of defensive, self-belittling remarks about his grades and his athletic skill. He offered excuses for his poor showing, at the same time denying that these were alibis. . . .

For Jack, competition was not some abstract thing that his father wanted. It was right in the family and its name was "Joe." In their father's long absences, Jack's big brother ruled the roost. Joe was bigger and heavier, more boisterous and outgoing than Jack. He demanded absolute obedience from the younger children in exchange for his brotherly help. Even today when asked whether anything really bothered him as child, Kennedy can think only of his big brother: "He had a pugnacious personality. Later on it smoothed out but it was a problem in my boyhood."

Jack was the only rival to Joe's throne; the next in line were girls and other boys too young to serve as more than nuisances. The two oldest boys often fought, and Jack always seemed to come off second. When the two boys raced around the block on their bicycles in opposite directions and collided head on, it was Jack who had to have twenty-eight stitches and Joe who emerged unscathed. Joe would throw a boy overboard for sloppy sailing in a race, and he would lie in wait to catch a rebellious brother—usually Jack—coming in off the breakwater. Bobby Kennedy to this day remembers cowering with his sisters upstairs while his older brothers fought furiously on the first floor.

The boys' father knew about the rivalry but it did not bother him, except when it got out of hands. He wanted competition in the family as long as the children stuck together in dealing with the world outside. He knew, too, that Joe Jr. made up for his bullying ways in generosity and kindness to his young brothers and sisters. Jack, too, for all his troubles at the hands of his older brother, feels today that Joe's overbearing ways, when later smoothed out, were one reason for his own success in school and in the war.

The family competition was not just physical. The father encouraged political argument at the dinner table, especially among himself and the older boys. He asserted his own views strongly, but though Jack says today that his father was sometimes rather harsh, he did not force his views on Joe, Jr. or on Jack. . . .

At eighteen, when he graduated from Choate, Jack Kennedy was a tall, thin, wiry boy with a narrow face, an almost snub nose, and a mop of hair that he tried unsuccessfully to control with hair tonic. He was good-looking but not as husky or as handsome as Joe, who had a square, open face, radiating Irish charm. . . .

Jack's first two years at Harvard were in some ways a duplicate of his life at Choate. Sports still excited him far more than studies. During his freshman year he tried out for football, swimming, and golf, and crowded in some softball, too. As he had at Choate, he played furiously but his drive was greater than his athletic skill. He was fearless and willing to fight until the game was over. He was plagued by illness, however, and he also injured his back at football, an injury that has followed him into adulthood.

Swimming was his passion and his best sport. A classmate recalls one occasion when Jack was hospitalized with a bad case of grippe just before he was to try out for a spot on the swimming squad that was to face Yale. Jack feared that the infirmary diet would leave him too weak to do well, so he persuaded his roommate to smuggle in steaks and chocolate malted milks. He sneaked out of the infirmary, swam furiously—and lost.

As a freshman, Jack took English, French, and history, and economics, and got C's in all except economics, where he earned a B. At the end of the year he was in the second lowest group of passing students. He did no better his sophomore year, receiving four C's, one D, and one B, though he concentrated in history and government and still read a good deal on his own, especially American history and biography. To his teachers he was a pleasant, bright, easygoing student. . . .

In his junior year, Kennedy began to come into his own. For one thing, Joe, Jr. graduated, bequeathing to Jack, incidentally, George Taylor, "gentleman's gentleman." Joe, Jr., more charming than ever, a born leader, gregarious, had played varsity football, won election to class offices, graduated with honors. True, he was now in Harvard Law School, but at least Jack was not completely in his shadow. Then, too, Jack particularly enjoyed rooming with Torbert Macdonald, a well-known Harvard football star.

Perhaps the most decisive step was Kennedy's trip with his friend Lem Billings to France, Spain, and Italy in the summer of 1937. He had traveled a good deal, but never as observantly as now. He had an audience with the Pope, and with Cardinal Pacelli, who inquired cordially after his father ("He is quite a fellow," Kennedy wrote home about the Cardinal); he saw a bullfight, climbed Vesuvius, and somehow talked his way into Monte Carlo with his bad French. "Played with my 5 fr. chips next to a woman who was playing $40.00 chips and she was quite upset about my winning 1.20 while she lost about $500.00," he reported to his father triumphantly. He talked with hitchhikers, reporters, diplomats. He found himself an admirer of the fascist corporate system in Italy, "as everyone seemed to like it in Italy." From Spain he wrote his father a dispassionate analysis of Britain's strategic stake in a victory for the Loyalists. . . .

Jack wrote his father that it was not so much what he learned abroad but the incentive it gave him to study when he got back that was important. If this was true, the incentive took more than a year to show up in his work at Harvard. But his grades did improve in his junior year; he became much more involved in studies, probably because they were now more directly related to the events he had seen in Europe. He was majoring in government, with emphasis on international relations. He read extensively in political theory—nationalism, fascism, and colonialism. He followed the newspapers closely; it was a time when political philosophers' doubts about the goodness of man and the future of the race seemed confirmed in the morning papers.

Solid, sound, earnest, but not brilliant—this is how his professors of government summed him up. "Kennedy is surprisingly able when he gets down to work," one of them noted. "His preparation may be spotty, but his general ability should bolster him up. A commendable fellow." He was affectionate, generous, and loyal to those who broke through his reserve, a reserve that was sometimes disguised as cockiness, sometimes as coolness.

At the end of 1937, when Jack was still in his sophomore year, President Roosevelt had suddenly appointed Joseph Kennedy ambassador to Britain. Many Boston aristocrats were aghast. Joe Kennedy, an Irishman and a Catholic, the envoy to the Court of St. James? The President must be mad. But, after all, they added bitterly, just what could you expect of a man who had deserted his class? And in East Boston the Irish were wondering, too. Imagine Pat Kennedy's boy all dressed up in satin knickers bowing before King George!

The most prized of all diplomatic posts, this ambassadorship put its occupant close to the top of the social world of two continents. For Joseph Patrick Kennedy it meant that after years of striving he had got about as far as he could hope to go. His position would also mean social preferment for his children. . . .

Moreover, Joseph Kennedy had reached a high station in his church. Father of a model Catholic family, husband of a deeply pious woman, he had contributed heavily to Catholic charities, hospitals, and other undertakings. He was on his way to being appointed a Knight of Malta and a Grand Knight of the Order of Pius IX. Yet there existed a dichotomy in his attitude toward the church. He had sent his daughters to Catholic schools, but not his sons. His daughters, he seemed to feel, should be trained the values and shaped by the character of the church. But his sons should have secular education to prepare them for the competitive struggle.

The family was increasingly dispersed geographically, but not psychologically. Some of the older children at their own request were godfather and godmother to the younger. The clan still gathered when it could on the Cape or in Palm Beach, playing parlor games and sports as fiercely as ever, and when the parents moved to London, Joe and Jack visited the embassy at Grosvenor Square as often as possible. About this time the father settled separate trust funds on each of his children amounting to well over a million dollars each. "I fixed it," he later told a reporter with a grin, "so that any of my children, financially speaking, could look me in the eye and tell me to go to hell." But he was mainly anxious as a speculator, to give them security against the vicissitudes of the future.

So, by the late 1930's, the Kennedys seemed to have everything—money, looks, education, brains, high standing in society, in their church, and in the nation. They were something new in America—the immigrants' final surpassing of the blue bloods. Yet something seemed missing. Perhaps it was that the family lacked roots. They seemed to live everywhere and nowhere. When the new Ambassador went to London, he simply added one more mansion to his homes in Florida and Massachusetts and his apartments and hotel suites in Boston and New York and Chicago and other way stations. The family had left Boston and the tenements far behind without identifying with any new locale or group. They were part of the New Deal upsurge but no longer emotionally kin to it, part of the highest income group but politically separated from it, moving in high social circles but not wholly accepted in them, worshippers in the Catholic Church but no will, at least on the part of the men, to submerge themselves in her.

It was this detachment, perhaps, that explains one of the most curious of Joseph Kennedy's actions—sending his beloved eldest boys to study in London under Harold Laski, who, as a Jew, a Socialist, an agnostic, a dogmatist, was at polar opposites from him. Only a man with absolute confidence that his sons would not fall for "political nostrums" would take such a chance. The father knew what he was doing. By the late '30's his son Joe held views that were almost a carbon copy of his father's— Democratic, but not New Deal, conservative socially, tending toward isolationism.

But, Jack? He was even less committed that his father or Joe. He seemed even more detached than the rest of the family. Alert, inquisitive, receptive, but somewhat remote, he looked at the world with quizzical gray eyes.

Chapter 2 THE STUDENT, THE WAR HERO, THE WRITER

ARTHUR M. SCHLESINGER, JR. (b. 1917)
holds the Albert Schweitzer Chair in the Humanities at the City University of New York.
He served as Special Assistant to President
Kennedy, and has written three books on the
Kennedys. In the following excerpt from his
highly-acclaimed *A Thousand Days*, what does
Schlesinger mean by JFK's "moral courage"?
What factors contributed to Kennedy's early
political education?

Kennedy was in and out of England in the months when Churchill was calling on his
fellow countrymen with such slight effect to rouse themselves against the menace of
Nazism. Harvard allowed him to spend the second term of the academic year of 1938–
39 abroad, and he traveled through Eastern Europe to Russia, the Middle East and the
Balkans, stopping in Berlin and Paris on his way back to Grosvenor Square. When he
returned to Harvard in the fall of 1939, the question of British somnambulism before
Hitler perplexed him more than ever. Professor Arthur Holcombe of the government
department had already aroused an interest in the study of politics: and now, under the
guidance of Professors Payson Wild and Bruce Hopper he set to work on an honors
essay analyzing British rearmament policy. After his graduation in 1940, the thesis
was published.

From *A Thousand Days: John F. Kennedy In The White House* by Arthur Schlesinger, Jr., copyright 1965.
Reprinted by permission of Houghton Mifflin Co., and Andre Deutsch, Ltd.

Remembering that Churchill had called his collection of speeches *While England Slept*, Kennedy brashly called his own book *Why England Slept*. In retrospect, *Why England Slept* presents several points of interest. One is its tone—so aloof and clinical, so different from the Churchillian history he loved, so skeptical of the notion that the individual could affect events. ("personalities," he wrote with regret about the American attitude toward history, "have always been more interesting to us than facts"). This detachment was all the more remarkable midst the flaring emotions of 1940. Though ostensibly writing to prepare America for its own crisis ("in studying the reasons why England slept, let us try to profit by them and save ourselves her anguish"), he remained agnostic about the choices confronting the American President. Kennedy did make the quiet suggestions that "a defeat of the Allies may simply be one more step towards the ultimate achievement—Germany over the world"; but, beyond this, and doubtless out of deference to his father's and older brother's isolationism, he stood aside in the book from the great debate between the isolationists and the interventionists. (At Harvard, however, he wrote to the *Crimson* criticizing the isolationist view of his fellow editors.)

His purpose was to discover how much British unpreparedness could be attributed to the personal defects of British politicians and how much to "the more general weakness of democracy and capitalism"; and he found his answer not with the leaders, but with the system. He declined to pursue guilty men: "Leaders are responsible for their failures only in the governing sector and cannot be held responsible for the nation as a whole . . . I believe it is one of democracy's failings that it seeks to make scapegoats for its own weaknesses." As long as Britain was a democracy, the people could have turned the leaders out if they disagreed with them. Nor did he put much stock in the notion that a leader could change the mind of the nation; after all, he remarked, Roosevelt had been trying to awaken America since 1937 but Congress was still cutting naval appropriations. The basic causes of the British paralysis in his view were impersonal and institutional. "In regard to capitalism, we observe first that it was obedience to its principles that contributed so largely to England's failure." Democracy, moreover, was "essentially peace-loving" and therefore hostile to rearmament. Both capitalism and democracy were geared for a world at peace; totalitarianism was geared for a world at war. A strong sense of the competition between democracy and totalitarianism pervaded the book—a competition in which, Kennedy believed, totalitarianism had significant short-run advantages, even though democracy was superior *"for the long run."*

As war came closer to America, Kennedy, having been rejected by the Army because of his back, succeeded in 1941 in persuading the Navy to let him in. After Pearl Harbor, he pulled every possible string to get sea duty, finally enrolling his father in the cause. In due course there followed the Pacific, PT-109, the Solomon Islands campaign, Talagi and Rendova, and the incredible few days in August 1945 when the Japanese destroyer *Amagiri* sliced his boat in half and plunged Kennedy and his crew into the waters of Ferguson Passage, now suddenly aflame with burning gasoline.

Kennedy's calm bravery, his extraordinary feat in towing one of his crew to refuge by gripping the end of the life jacket belt in his teeth, his leadership, resourcefulness and cheer until rescue came—this was one of the authentic passages of heroism in the war so well described in later accounts by John Hersey and Robert Donovan and so seldom mentioned by Kennedy himself. (In a Person to Person program with Edward R. Murrow in the late fifties, Kennedy called it "an interesting experience." Murrow responded: "Interesting. I should think that would be one of the great understatements." When during the Presidency Donovan proposed doing a book on PT-109, Kennedy tried his best to discourage him, saying that there was no story and it would be a waste of his time. Donovan went ahead nevertheless and eventually decided that he would have to go out to the Solomons and reswim Kennedy's course. Kennedy, who thought this utter madness, could not get over the idea anyone's going to such trouble and expense.)

The incident in the Solomons embodied two of Kennedy's deeper preoccupations—with courage and with death. He hated discussing these matters in the abstract, but they were nonetheless enduring themes of his life. Robert Kennedy tells us that courage was the virtue his brother most admired. In the first instance, this meant physical courage—the courage of men under enemy fire, of men silently suffering pain, the courage of the sailor and the mountain climber and of men who stared down mobs or soared into outer space. And, when he entered politics, it came to mean moral courage—the courage to which he later dedicated his *Profiles*, the courage of "a man who does what he must—in spite of personal consequences, in spite of obstacles and dangers and pressures," the courage which, he said, "is the basis of all human morality."

Courage—and death. The two are related, because courage, if it is more than reckless bravado, involves the exquisite understanding that death may be its price. "The education of the average American child of the upper middle class," Norbert Wiener has written, "is such as to guard him solicitously against the awareness of death and doom." But this is less true of children brought up in an orthodox faith. Kennedy's religious upbringing, his illness, his reading about the death of kings—all must have joined to give him an early sense of human mortality. Then death became his intimate during the long hours in the black, streaming waters of Ferguson Passage. Exactly a year later, he was notified that his brother Joe had been killed on an air mission against Nazi submarine bases in western Europe. In another month his English brother-in-law, the Marquis of Hartington, the husband of his sister Kathleen, was killed in France.

In a looseleaf notebook of 1945, filled with fragments about Joe and Billy Hartington—Joe's posthumous citation, a *Washington Post* editorial on his death, Kathleen's letter about her husband's death and letters from Billy Hartington's fellow officers in the Coldstream Guards—he inserted two quotations describing the death of Raymond Asquith in France in 1915—one of Churchill's *Great Contemporaries*:

The War which found the measure of so many men never got to the bottom of him, and when the Grenadiers strode into the crash and thunder of Somme, he went to his fate, cool, poised, resolute, matter-of-fact, debonair.

and another from a favorite book, John Buchan's *Pilgrim's Way*:

He loved his youth, and his youth has become eternal. Debonair and brilliant and brave, he is part of that immortal England which knows not age or weariness or defeat.

His wife later said, "The poignancy of men dying young haunted him."

Along with a deep sorrow over the battalions of wasted lives, the war left him with an intense concern about the prevention of such waste in the future. He went to San Francisco in June 1945 as a special writer for the Hearst press to watch the founding of the United Nations. For a young veteran, with stabbing memories of violence and death, it was in a way a disenchanting experience. But for a student of politics it was an indispensable education.

"It would be very easy to write a letter to you that was angry," he observed afterward to a PT-boat friend who had sought his opinion of the conference. "When I think of how much this war has cost us, of the deaths of Cy and Peter and Orv and Gil and Demi and Joe and Billy and all of those thousands and millions who have died with them—when I think of all those gallant acts that I have seen or anyone has seen who has been to the war—it would be a very easy thing to feel disappointed and somewhat betrayed." The conference, he continued, lacked moral force; not idealism but self-interest brought the nations together. "You have seen battlefields where sacrifice was the order of the day and to compare that sacrifice to the timidity and selfishness of the nations gathered at San Francisco must inevitably be disillusioning."

Yet could the conference have achieved more? The hard fact was that nations were not prepared to yield their sovereignty to an international organization. He listened in the corridors to the world government arguments of another young veteran, Cord Meyer, about to start the World Federalists. "Admittedly world organization with common obedience to law would be solution," Kennedy scribbled in a notebook. "Not that easy. If there is not the feeling that war is the ultimate evil, a feeling strong enough to drive them together, then you can't work out this internationalist plan." "Things cannot be forced from the top," he told his PT-boat friend.

The international relinquishing of sovereignty would have to spring from the people—it would have to be so strong that the elected delegates could be turned out of office if they failed to do it. . . . We must face the truth that the people have not been horrified by war to a sufficient extent to force them to go to any extent rather than have another war. . . . War will exist until that distant day when the conscientious objector enjoys the same reputation and prestige that the warrior does today.

These were the thing to be considered "when you consider the Conference in San Francisco. You must measure its accomplishments against its possibilities. What [the] Conference accomplished is that it made war more difficult." He summed up his feelings about the UN in his notebook:

> *Danger of too great a build-up*
> Mustn't expect too much.
> A truly just solution will leave every nation somewhat disappointed. There is no cure all.

This was his mood immediately after the war: don't expect too much: no cure-alls. The next year he wrote succinctly in the six-year report of the Harvard Class of 1940, "I joined the Navy in 1941, served in P. T. Boats in the Pacific and was retired in April, 1945, because of injuries." (The Class Secretary added a footnote: "Kennedy received the Navy and Marine Corps Medal.") Concluding a brief paragraph, Kennedy replied to a question asked all members of the class, "I am pessimistic about the future of the country."

He had expected to become a writer; but the San Francisco experience may have helped persuade him that it was better to sit at the conference table than to wait outside with the press. His brother's death also changed things. The family assumption had been that Joe, who had made his political debut as a delegate at the 1940 Democratic convention (where he cast his vote, as pledged, against Franklin Roosevelt), would be the Kennedy to enter politics. Though Ambassador Kennedy did not, as myth later had it, automatically promote his second son into the slot now so sadly vacant, Jack like many young veterans, felt the need of doing something to help the world for which so many friends had died. Politics perhaps attracted him less as a means of saving this world than of keeping it from getting worse. In 1946 he returned to Boston to test the political air.

Chapter 3 THE KENNEDYS IN ANOTHER LIGHT

CLAY BLAIR, JR. (b. 1925) has written extensively and served as editor in chief of the Curtis Publishing Company. He and his wife Joan (b. 1929) were the first to challenge, with meticulous research, the traditional, family-assisted accounts of the Kennedys. In the following, from the landmark *The Search For J.F.K.*, what insights into Kennedy and his parents seem especially important? What sort of man does JFK appear to be?

Joe Kennedy was an immensely complicated character. In business he was shrewd, ruthless, and unscrupulous, believing contemptuously that "all businessmen were sons-of-bitches" (as Jack reported when he was President). He made his money in liquor, cheap movies, racetracks, gambling in the stock market (even rigging stocks on occasion), and real estate. He was a Catholic, yet amoral: his love affairs were conducted almost publicly. Not many people liked Joe Kennedy. Not a few believed he was a crook. The Boston Establishment ostracized him and that was why he moved away. . . .

When most of his children were young, he was almost an absentee father—off in New York, Hollywood, Washington. He was not even present for the birth of several of his children. And yet, he took a deep interest in his children. He encouraged them in

From *The Search For J.F.K.* by Clay and Joan Blair, Jr., copyright 1977. Reprinted by permission of The Berkeley Publishing Group.

sports, planned their education, urged them to seize higher social ground. He set up $1 million trust funds for them when they reached the age of twenty-one, then pointed them toward public service. When he was home, he ruled the roost absolutely. . . .

Rose was also a complex person. She was petite, gentle, intelligent. When her children were young she was able to devote most of her hours exclusively to them, because there were always plenty of domestics to handle housekeeping chores. She stimulated their interest in history and saw to their religious upbringing. Each was sent away to boarding school at an appropriate age; it was the custom of those who could afford it. She loved to travel and as the children entered boarding school, she traveled almost constantly. She was devoutly religious, a daily communicant, who contributed much time (and money) to various Catholic organizations and causes. She took care of her relatives when they fell on hard times. She was notoriously absentminded, always pinning reminder notes to her dress or leaving them around the house in strategic locations. She took pride in her figure, and her clothes were the latest Paris fashions. Yet she was extremely frugal in mundane matters, such as the household budget, an eccentricity she passed along to all her children. She neither drank nor smoked.

In her reflections [*Times to Remember*, published in 1974] Rose had nothing but the kindest words for her husband. She innocently dismisses his notorious affair with [actress] Gloria Swanson by describing the relationship as a complicated business deal. She is not critical of his long absences from home in the early years, including the times when she was giving birth, because, she says, he was off working hard for the family. . . . Rose is certainly entitled to remember what she wants the way she wants. But our view is that Rose was roughly treated by her husband, who had little or no respect for women. As we see it, she escaped into an intensely religious, near-fantasy life, a life of distracting travel and withdrawals to her private retreats at Hyannis Port and elsewhere. We think it noteworthy that in her book many of the recollections of the children growing up are supplied by the children themselves; and that when important or tragic family events occurred, she was often off somewhere else.

From his mother Jack acquired an interest in history. At her encouragement he became a voracious reader of books—history, biography, romantic literature. (*King Arthur and the Round Table, The Jungle Book, Kidnapped, Arabian Nights,* and so on.) The reading led to his knack for writing. She passed on her religion; Jack kept the Sacraments and attended church on Sundays and Holy Days, though clearly he was not nearly so devout as she. Later, he even considered giving up Catholicism. Finally, we believe, Jack inherited or acquired from his mother her peculiar absentmindedness. He was extremely disorganized, always leaving clothes, briefcases, or papers behind in hotels or airports or on trains. He was late for appointments and often forgot them altogether. . . .

To Ambassador Kennedy, life was a game to be won, whatever the cost. Perhaps this view extended to women as well: they were to be "won" against other male competitors; and displayed. As trophies, the women had to be glossy.

We asked Betty Spalding, the most introspective and brightest of Jack's female friends, what she thought about Jack's relationship with women. She considered the question for a long time, then said:

Jack and I had a warm brother-sister relationship. A very long association that way. He would say personal things to me. I mean, ask me personal questions about women and marriage—and later he talked to me about his sex life with Jackie. This was a rare relationship, I think. He was not the kind of person to have self-revealing conversations. Jack had a total lack of ability to relate, emotionally, to anyone. Everything was so surface with him in his relationships with people. All of the Kennedys were blocked, totally blocked, emotionally. Eunice survived best. I don't know how or why. Knowing the old man and Mrs. Kennedy, spending so much time in the house, I can readily see the limitations.

Mrs. Kennedy, for all her kids, was not a mother, not a homebody, but a driving, dominating force. And the old man—having his mistresses there at the house for lunch and supper! I couldn't understand it! It was unheard of.

Betty Spalding would not be the only Kennedy friend to tell us the ambassador brought his mistresses into the Kennedy home. In fact, it became a routine "revelation" as the friends attempted to explain the ambassador's character and his relationship with Rose.

Betty Spalding went on:

I think that was one of the things that was so difficult for Jack when he finally married Jackie. Both of them were blocked emotionally. She had the same emotional blocks and panics that Jack had. And their relationship was extremely stormy at the beginning. But it was getting better. They were both growing up emotionally. You see, there's something about the emotional imprintings of people. If they don't go through their proper psychosexual emotional development corresponding to their chronological age, they're going to go through those developments sometime, as late bloomers.

The first I ever saw Jack able to relate was when he had Caroline. That was a marvelous relationship. He was able to release some of his emotions to her and it freed him from the fear of it and he was able to exchange better with Jackie and she with him. Until he had Caroline, he never really learned how to deal with people. It was the first time he ever revealed any kind of emotion. It was fascinating to watch him grow in this capacity.

But, as I said, in the early years, he was not able to emotionally relate to anyone. His friends—the people around him—were followers and worshippers—Lem Billings, Torby Macdonald. They were all servile and subservient. He compartmented his friends. And I think that is part and parcel of his inability to relate to people. . . .

In these years [1935–1947], Jack had two distinct, compartmentalized (that is, nonassociating) sets of male friends: political associates and personal friends. Leaving aside the political associates (a special case), we see that most of his close pals—Lem Billings, Rip Horton, Charlie Houghton, Ben Smith, Torby Macdonald, Chuck Spalding, Red Fay, and Jim Reed—were remarkably like Jack, from the same Eastern prep schools (except Fay), and Ivy League milieu. They were bright, gregarious, amusing, and fun-loving. Most came from more financially modest backgrounds, but none sought personal gain through Jack's money. Most (five of these eight) were non-Catholic. Some were notorious womanizers. Most were athletes, with a compelling interest in sports. All were, in these years, conservative politically. None was "intellectual" in the strictest definition. Jack was the dominant figure of the group; the others were satellites revolving around Jack. Most were willing to do almost anything he proposed. All were intensely loyal to Jack.

And what of Jack's relationship with the opposite sex? Does it tell us anything about Jack in these years? We think it does. As Betty Spalding, Cis McLaughlin, Mary Pitcairn and others close to the Kennedy family in these years told us, there was clearly a strained, if not bizarre, emotional relationship between Joe and Rose Kennedy. And, as we have seen in Jack's letters to Rip Horton's first wife, Jane, and to Red Fay, Jack, in spite of all this religious indoctrination to the contrary, grew up with a chary, if not cynical, view of "love" and marriage. He worried how it might upset existing male relationships. He was, as Betty said, "emotionally blocked," incapable of a deep and lasting relationship with a woman. Many young men of those days grew up with similar reserve, but Jack's was, we believe, exceptional, perhaps extreme.

His outlook about women may have been affected significantly by his college-days love affair with Frances Ann Cannon. . . . Whatever the case, as Jack grew to manhood, marriage was far from his mind and would remain so until age thirty-six. As Jim Reed, Chuck Spalding, and Kay Stammers Menzies told us, and as Kick [Jack's sister Kathleen] wrote in a letter to Jack in 1943, Jack had adopted the "British view" of women. That is, he enjoyed foremost the manly companionship of his male friends. Women were secondary and primarily sex objects. He relished the chase, the conquest, the testing of himself, the challenge of numbers and quality. . . .

Jack, as we were told, relished his reputation as a ladies' man, both in these young years and (as everybody must know by now) in later years, including his married years and White House years. It is our inclination to find this womanizing unattractive—but it must be said that he didn't coerce or deceive any of these women, and judging from their loyalty to him, none of them felt damaged by their relationships with him. . . .

Let us here recapitulate the other major omissions and distortions of Jack's public image.

First, the impression was given that Jack was a robust young man. As we have seen in countless examples in these pages, the exact opposite is true. His health, almost from birth, was disastrously poor. He was born with an unstable back which progressively deteriorated throughout his life, necessitating first a brace or "corset" and, later, two spinal operations. It is a distortion—or a downright lie—to attribute his bad back to either a Harvard football injury or the PT-109. Even if he had not engaged in these strenuous exertions, the back would have failed. Throughout his childhood, and especially during our period, 1935–1947, he was tormented by an almost continuous series of illnesses, most of which we were unable to identify because the medical records are still closed. In his junior year at Choate, a "severe illness" significantly impaired his schoolwork. Another illness (or a recurrence of this one) forced him to lose a full year of college in 1935–1936. He was ill during many of his Harvard years. He collapsed in London in September, 1937. He was ill during the spring, summer, and fall of 1938. In 1940, after graduation from Harvard, Mayo Clinic physicians advised him to take another academic year off to recover his health. At the end of the year he was back in hospitals for extended periods. He did not pass the Navy physical by doing five months of back-strengthening exercises. His father pulled strings to get him by the Navy physical. After a mere six months of active duty, he had to request six months inactive duty for health reasons. According to Lennie Thom [a friend and fellow sailor], he arrived in the Solomons in poor health. Seven or eight months later, he was relieved of command of the PT-59 on orders of a doctor, and wound up in a hospital in the Solomons. He spent most of his last year in the Navy—1944—in and out of hospitals and finally, was surveyed out of the Navy because of his health. Again, in 1945, he returned to Arizona planning to spend a full year recovering his health. He gave that up—but again collapsed in London. In the fall of 1945 he faced another (unspecified) operation, evidently not performed. In his 1946 race for the House he was in constant poor health (and suffered severely from back pains), collapsing in the final Charlestown parade. In 1947 he again collapsed in London—with Addison's disease. It is a distortion—or downright lie—to attribute any of Jack's postwar illness (including the cover story "malaria") to his PT service in the Solomon Islands.

Second, the impression was fostered that Jack was a dedicated and brilliant scholar. Here again we believe the exact opposite to be true. At Choate he was clearly a sloppy, lazy, and uninterested student. At Harvard, he was more interested in athletics than scholarship until his senior year, when he turned with an uncharacteristic burst of energy to write his thesis. In this period he did not ever again demonstrate any large capacity for study. The thesis itself was mediocre. The book that emerged from it, *Why England Slept*, was the product of many hands: the embassy staff, faculty advisers, Arthur Krock and Joe Kennedy. Its publication heightened the impression that Jack was a scholarly intellectual with a natural talent for writing. But, as we have shown, there is little evidence to support this.

Writing and scholarly investigations are disciplines that demand long, lonely, patient years of solitude and reflection. We do not think Jack was intellectually or temperamentally suited for either. He was not a reflective man. He was an activist, living life (like all the Kennedys) at a frenetic pace, racing for planes, trains, steamers, lunch, dinner, the theater. We could not possibly imagine Jack forswearing that life for one in the Ivory Tower. And, of course, he did not. He was certainly very bright, but he was a "quick study," not an intellectual or scholar.

His studies at The London School of Economics and at Stanford University are cited by some authors and journalists as further proof of his scholarly dedication. As we have seen, he did not even attend The London School of Economics. The ninety-day stint (always reported as a full semester) at Stanford was a lark.

In the same vein, the assertion by many authors that Jack Kennedy seriously embarked on a promising career in journalism in 1945, then rejected it for politics, is also clearly wrong. As we have seen, it was Jack's father who put this scheme in motion, a temporary assignment for Hearst newspapers to keep Jack's name before the public and get him credentials to travel in Europe. His five thousand words of journalism (this time without Krock's skillful fingers) was a dismal performance, on a par with the output of any cub reporter. He did not, as widely reported, brilliantly predict Churchill's defeat. On the contrary, he wrongly predicted Churchill's reelection.

Third, the impression was assiduously nurtured that Jack was a war hero. As we have recounted in no small detail, the evidence does not support the claim. Skipping directly to the Solomon Islands and PT-109, once again let us encapsulate the provable facts. Between July 15 and July 31, during about two weeks in combat, the 109 made about seven patrols. On none of these nights did the 109 have contact with or fire at enemy surface forces. On three nights, the 109's section was attacked by Japanese float planes. On one of these attacks two of Jack's ten-man enlisted crew were injured and hospitalized. On the night of August 12, going on her eighth patrol, the 109 was part of a fifteen-boat flotilla deployed to intercept a specific group of Japanese destroyers at a specific place. When the destroyers appeared, precisely as predicted, Jack failed to follow prescribed procedure, did not follow his section leader to attack. Moreover, when the section leader suffered a "flash" in his torpedo tube, drawing heavy enemy fire, Jack left him to his fate. Two or three hours later, when the destroyers returned, again as expected, the 109 had a second chance to attack. But this time she was carelessly disposed for combat. Two men, Harris and Johnston, were asleep; two others, Thom and Kirksey, were lying down on the deck—unalert. The radioman, Maguire, was in the cockpit, not at his radio where he should have been. In clear violation of standard combat procedure and common sense (as Jack later conceded in the classified PT newspaper), the 109 had only one of its three engines engaged. Although other PTs spotted phosphorescent wakes from a mile or more away, the 109 did not see an onrushing ship until it was on top of them. Two men died in the collision; two others were badly burned. All in all, the evidence to this point suggests that (as some expressed it to us) Jack Kennedy was far from being a PT hero.

Contrary to all published reports of the six-day survival episode (including that in [James MacGregor] Burns) prior to his inauguration as president, Jack did not "save" his crew. It is not true, as reported by John Hersey and others, that the PT base gave up hope and launched no rescue operation. The opposite it true. It was the PT base alert to—and continued pressure on—the coastwatcher [Arthur] Evans and his native rescue apparatus that ultimately resulted in the rescue of the crew. The famous coconut message was far less comprehensive and helpful than the message written with a pencil on very prosaic paper by Lennie Thom. The very existence of a Thom message was not made known until Jack was already in the White House. He surely saved one life—[Patrick] McMahon's—and he performed bravely, but more impulsively than intelligently and not in the least effectively, in making his nighttime swims for help. His failure to fire the Very pistol [a flare gun] surely led to the men being "lost" for a week in the first place.

Each of the three officers on PT-109 (Kennedy, Thom, Ross) were awarded minor medals for "heroism" for their performances during the postcollision and survival phase. As we have shown, there is good reason to doubt the authenticity of some of the medal citations. We do not understand why there are *two* extant citations for Jack's medal. The enlisted men, some of whom "saved" more men than the officers, received no medals.

As we have reported, it was wartime censorship and Joe Kennedy's contacts at *Reader's Digest* that were primarily responsible for Jack receiving so much credit during this episode. He was, in effect, a "manufactured" war hero. Here, we believe, the Washington Press Corps deserves a failing grade. It blindly accepted Jack's version of his combat record, or the incomplete, censored wartime accounts, with no independent investigation. It was not until Jack was already president that Robert Donovan told the full story, and even then he distorted certain portions of it to put Jack in a more favorable light.

Finally, there is this question: Do these omissions and distortions matter? We believe that they constitute overwhelming evidence that shrewd manipulation of the media can make a man president of the United States.

Chapter 4 MIND AND CHARACTER

THEODORE C. SORENSEN (b. 1928) was
JFK's long-time confidant and speech writer.
Today he is a New York attorney and remains
active in the Democratic Party. The following,
from *Kennedy*, contains Sorensen's assess-
ments of JFK's mind and character. How
would you describe Kennedy's "extraordinary
growth"?

I cannot single out any one day as the time I began to understand John Kennedy as a
human being. Gradually I discovered that the simplicity of this man's tastes and
demeanor was, while genuine, deceptive as well as disarming. Although he possessed
·unusual empathy, and a remarkable sense of what was fitting and appropriate for every
kind of occasion, he never "put on an act," feigning anger or joy when he did not feel
it. Nevertheless his hidden qualities outnumbered the apparent. The freshman Senator
from Massachusetts, with all his "ordinary" ways, was an enormously complex and
extraordinarily competent man.

   I came to marvel at his ability to look at his own strengths and weaknesses with
utter detachment, his candid and objective responses to public questions, and his

From *Kennedy* by Theodore C. Sorensen, pages 13, 14, 16, 21, 22, 23, 27, 28. Copright © 1965 by
Theodore C. Sorensen. Reprinted by permission of Harper & Row, Publishers, Inc. and Hodder &
Stoughton Ltd.

insistence on cutting through prevailing bias and myths to the heart of a problem. He had a disciplined and analytical mind. Even his instincts, which were sound, came from his reason rather than his hunches. He hated no enemy, he wept at no adversity. He was neither willing nor able to be flamboyant or melodramatic.

But I also learned in time that this cool, analytical mind was stimulated by a warm, compassionate heart. Beneath the careful pragmatic approach lay increasingly deep convictions on basic goals and unusual determination to achieve them. "Once you say you're going to settle for second," he said in 1960 regarding the Vice Presidency, "that's what happens to you in life, I find." Jack Kennedy never settled for second if first was available. . . .

The more one knew John Kennedy, the more one liked him. And those of us who came to know him well—though we rarely heard him discuss his personal feelings—came to know the strength and warmth of his dedication as well as his logic. As John Buchan wrote of a friend in John Kennedy's favorite book, *Pilgrim's Way*, "He disliked emotion, not because he felt lightly but because he felt deeply." John Kennedy could always look at himself objectively and laugh at himself wholeheartedly—and those two rare gifts enabled him to talk lightly while feeling deeply. As he said himself about Robert Frost, "His sense of the human tragedy fortified him against self-deception and easy consolation."

There were other qualities beneath the surface. Under that seemingly fortunate and gay exterior lay an acute awareness of the most sobering kinds of tragedy. He lived with the memory of a much admired older brother [Joe Junior] killed in the war and the memory of a sister [Kathleen] killed in a plane crash overseas. Add to this a history of illness, pain and injury since childhood, and the fact that another sister [Rosemary] was confined to a home for the mentally retarded, and one understands his human sensitivity. No mention was ever made of any of these subjects by the Senator. But his familiarity with tragedy had produced in him both a desire to enjoy the world and a desire to improve it; and these two desires, particularly in the years preceding 1953, had sometimes been in conflict.

His mental processes—so direct and clear-cut in conversation—were not uncomplicated either. He was at that time considered with some disdain to be an intellectual by most Massachusetts politicians and considered with equal disdain to be a politician by most Massachusetts intellectuals. . . .

Although by the time we met in 1953 he had achieved considerable success as a politician, he had no grandiose picture of himself as a chosen savior of mankind from any specific evil. But he did recognize, with his customary objectivity that put both modesty and ego aside, that he possessed abilities, ideals and public appeal which could be combined to help the nation with whatever problems it faced. In all the years that followed, however the problems and his public image may have changed, that private vision of himself and his role never altered. . . .

We had different ideological backgrounds, and most of the professional liberals were slow to warm to him. But I found that he was the truest and oldest kind of liberal:

the free man with the free mind. He entered Congress, he freely admitted, with little or no political philosophy. The aggressive attitudes of many "professional liberals" made him "uncomfortable". . . .

Kennedy had seen that many devotees of the left as well as the right could be rigid and dogmatic in their views, parroting the opinions of their respective political and intellectual leaders without reflection or re-examination. . . .

When asked which kind of President he hoped to be, liberal or conservative, he replied, "I hope to be responsible." Perhaps his wife summed him up best as "an idealist without illusions."

As Senator, candidate and President, his tests were: Can it work? Can it help? And, often but not always: Can it pass? He could grasp the essence of a complex subject with amazing speed, and his natural instincts were almost always on the progressive side of an issue. But his natural caution required him to test those instincts against evidence and experience. This realistic emphasis on the possible induced critics and commentators to describe him as a pragmatist, which for the most part he was. To be reminded by daily disappointments that he lived in an imperfect world did not surprise or depress him, but he cared enough about the future of that world never to be satisfied with the present. Indeed, in his campaign and in the White House, his analyses of conditions in his country and planet consistently began with those four words: "I am not satisfied . . . .".

Some might say that he fiddled around as a Congressman and really didn't become interested until his sophomore year in the Senate. It seemed to me in 1953 that an inner struggle was being waged for the spirit of John Kennedy—a struggle between the political dilettante and the statesman, between the lure of luxury and lawmaking. His performance in the House of Representatives had been considered by most observers to be largely undistinguished—except for a record of absenteeism which had been heightened by indifference as well as ill health and by unofficial as well as official travels.

Having won a Senate seat and a satisfactory measure of glory, he had proved his worth in his chosen profession of politics. It was six years until re-election, and the responsibilities of a freshman Democratic Senator under a Republican Congress and administration were neither weighty nor exciting. Having borne more pain and gloom than he liked to remember, he enjoyed in his bachelor days carefree parties and companions on both sides of the Atlantic Ocean. There was a natural temptation to spend the limited number of days in which he could count on enjoying full health in pursuit of pleasure as well as duty.

But gradually the statesman won out, as his convictions deepened, his concerns broadened and Washington and the world occupied more and more of his time. And as clear as the fact the fact of John Kennedy's extraordinary growth is the fact that many factors contributed to it: his reading, his traveling, and the widening scope of his associates, experiences and responsibilities.

In 1952 he was elected to the United States Senate, broadening his concerns as well as his constituency.

In 1953 he was married, ending the carefree life of the bachelor and establishing a home of his own.

In 1954 a spinal operation brought him close to death, and the long months of immobile recuperation were spent in sober reflection.

In 1955 he learned, as he researched and wrote a book, about the essence of democracy, the public office-holder's relations with his public.

In 1956 he narrowly missed the Vice Presidential nomination of his party, emerging as a national figure in wide demand.

In 1957–1959 he crisscrossed the country constantly, campaigning in areas wholly unlike his own, observing as well as orating, learning as well as teaching.

In 1960 he was successively Presidential candidate, Presidential nominee and President-elect, and the increased horizons and responsibilities of each role increased the breadth and depth of his perception.

In 1961 the Presidency altered his outlook and insight even more.

Chapter 5 THE CONGRESSMAN, THE AUTHOR

HERBERT S. PARMET (b. 1929) is professor of history at Queensborough Community College and the Graduate School of the City University of New York. His *Jack: The Struggles Of John F. Kennedy* was widely praised for its objectivity. In this excerpt, Parmet examines the controversial issue of JFK's physical health and questions his claim to being a writer. Is the discussion of *Profiles In Courage* persuasive?

[By October, 1947, when it was diagnosed in London] Jack Kennedy was a victim of Addison's Disease. Addison's has several manifestations. Mostly, the disease impairs the excretion of the adrenal glands, reducing the patient's immunity to illness. Weakness, loss of weight (which would explain the reduction Jack had experienced), loss of appetite, pigmentation of exposed skin, and most seriously of course, a mortality rate that resulted from almost inevitable infections that the body could not fight. Surgery, however minor, could easily be fatal. At the Lahey Clinic in Boston, he was treated by Dr. Elmer Bartels, a thyroid specialist. Kennedy remained under the doctor's close care, visiting him on at least April 3, 1948, January 29, 1949, and

From *Jack: The Struggles Of John F. Kennedy* by Herbert S. Parmet, copyright © 1980 by Herbert S. Parmet. Reprinted by permission of Doubleday, a division of Bantam Doubleday Dell Publishing Group, Inc., and Russell & Volkening.

August 4, 1949. During this entire period he often commuted to Boston and New York for medical reasons. And in May of 1955 Kennedy came under the care of Dr. Janet Travell, a New York pharmacologist with an office at 9 West Sixteenth Street. But by that time the most serious implications of Addison's Disease had been largely overcome.

Nevertheless, whispers about the condition plagued Kennedy for many years, always threatening public revelation, with all the horrors of a dreaded disease that would inevitably preclude any political responsibility. When revelations about Addison's could no longer be stilled, especially after John Connally, acting in the interests of Lyndon Johnson, made the charge just before the 1960 Democratic convention prepared to select its candidates, efforts were made to counter the alarming political consequences. A typical example of the "official" explanation appears in Arthur Schlesinger Jr.'s *A Thousand Days*. Although published after his death, readers were told that Jack Kennedy did not have Addison's in the classic sense—that is, caused by turberculosis of the adrenal glands—that he had not had tuberculosis in any form and that, with modern methods of treatment, his adrenal insufficiency— evidently induced by the long night of swimming during the PT 109 episode, and the subsequent malaria—presented no serious problem.

Nevertheless, a detailed medical report, published in the *Archive of Surgery*, described Kennedy as having a "marked adrenocortical insufficiency," which rendered his subsequent back operations hazardous. Joseph Alsop, who saw a great deal of Kennedy at his Georgetown home, a welcome retreat from problems, remembers that some of the doctors at first suspected that he had Hodgkin's Disease, which would have been fatal. Moreover, Addison's itself, left to the treatment then available, would have severely reduced the patient's longevity. Kennedy told Alsop that he expected to die in his early forties.

"The doctors say I've got a sort of slow-motion leukemia, but they tell me I'll probably last until I'm forty-five," Schlesinger quoted him telling Alsop at one point. That was how Jack chose to explain his Addison's.

In such conversations, Kennedy appeared wryly fatalistic and gave the impression of little desire except to live out whatever time remained. Alsop got the feeling that he "really did not remember clearly political events between the time he came to Congress and when he found ambition. Until then, he did what his father wanted him to do without paying much attention." A close family friend recalled that, at that time, Jack "was good and sick. And so sick that it was an irritation for both of them, for his father and for himself. It threatened to get in the way of everything they were trying to accomplish."

Furthermore, the medical report left no doubt that Kennedy's Addison's Disease, contrary to the information given to unwary biographers, was a "classic" case, one that required the standard treatment. Namely, daily injections of desoxycorticosterone acetate pellets (DOCA). Such pellets, 150 mg strong, were then implanted in Jack Kennedy's thighs. That required, according to Joan and Clay Blair, the maintenance of "safe-deposit boxes around the country containing cortisone and DOCA so that Jack would never run out."

The real godsend was the arrival of cortisone in a form that could be taken orally. Its effect was dramatic, remarkably contributing to not only the patient's stamina but to his sense of well-being—even to his sexual appetites. There were side effects for someone on so high a daily maintenance as was Kennedy (25 mg), side effects that medical authorities warn can damage other parts of the system and cause added weight and facial puffiness. . . .

Those who ran Joe Kennedy's New York office, including [former Harvard Law School Dean James] Landis and all his associates, constituted a formidable behind-the-scenes unofficial staff in behalf of Jack Kennedy, one quite apart from any public payroll.

Nothing about it was irregular. It merely emulated other officeholders who had private means that enabled them to hire personal staffs and reach out for endless advisers. The Kennedy machinery, however, was distinctive in one vital respect: the continuing role of the Ambassador. Jack Kennedy's physical condition obviously made such assistance invaluable. It kept him dependent and impaired his ability to exert a freer and personally more satisfying role. He had to tolerate the circumstances he described soon after taking his congressional seat when he told newspaperwoman Elizabeth Oldfield that "for a long time I was Joseph P. Kennedy's son, then I was Kathleen's brother, then Eunice's brother." Then he added, "Some day I hope to be able to stand on my own feet."

There were many such comments, mostly made in private asides to close friends. All were submerged behind the facade of Kennedy family unity. Additionally, the Ambassador himself, who was sufficiently astute to understand the potentially counterproductive nature of his efforts, chose to minimize his own visibility. He hired aides. He expedited. He utilized contacts, official and unofficial. Joe Kennedy understood the distinctions between the political realities within the Eleventh District of Massachusetts and ideological satisfaction. Not that the Ambassador was an ideologue, at least in the ordinary sense. But his position conveyed the visceral responses of the successful businessman, confident that the rest of the world can also profit from his genius. . . .

Park Avenue had long since become the headquarters of the Kennedy enterprises, first at number 270 and later at 230. In that New York nerve center, Landis was ensconced with his own staff. There, in addition to servicing the complex financial and legal needs of his employer (including the preparation of the Ambassador's memoirs), Landis oversaw drafts of proposed articles for publication under the congressman's signature, ideas for legislation, the gathering of background material to assist the Washington office, and made suggestions for political responses pertaining to a wide variety of matters. The central directive was simple enough: Do whatever could help Jack's career. . . .

With the help of whatever supportive apparatus his father could muster, Jack

Kennedy had become an adequate congressman, displaying flashes of talent, ingratiating himself here and there, but mainly seeming lethargic and bored. Obediently, he was going through the motions of fulfilling the role of replacing Joe Junior. Outsiders, unaware of the family mission, had little reason to predict a productive future. As the Representative from the Eleventh of Massachusetts, he duly compromised notions of classical liberalism by delivering on the so-called bread-and-butter issues. Without much concern for civil liberties, he rivaled most colleagues and appeased contituents by exploiting the national obsession over anticommunism. Yet, he remained an independent force, not showing much regard for partisan obligations within the Commonwealth or on Capitol Hill. He was a young man who failed to convince others that he had much ambition or clarity about his goals. While he hardly appeared robust, few realized the seriousness of his physical condition. Before the miracle of cortisone, the prospect of an early death kept him from trying very hard to develop either his ability or hereditary gifts for much more than having a good time. His attendance record was among the worst in the House. What was the sense if he was not going to survive his forties. . . .

On December 18, 1955, while Dr. Travell was with him at Palm Beach, *The New Tork Times Magazine* featured an article by John F. Kennedy called "The Challenge of Political Courage," adapted, readers were advised, from his forthcoming book, *Profiles in Courage*. Indeed, when he had returned to the Senate in May, he had revealed for the first time that a book was in progress. Newspapers explained that Jack Kennedy was working on a "history" of the United States Senate.

Published at the start of 1956, *Profiles in Courage* found a receptive audience and no shortage of reviewers. From *The New York Times* and New York *Herald Tribune* to more obscure publications, commentators fell into line, generally praising the work for its thoughtful, inspirational examples of courage within the Senate. In a major front-page discussion in *The New York Times Book Review*, which featured a large picture of a dignified, serious-looking Jack Kennedy, Cabell Phillips declared satisfaction at having a "first-rate politican write a thoughtful and persuasive book about political integrity" and went on to praise the author for being "no dilettante at his trade, but a solid journeyman full of ideals, but few illusions. His book," concluded Phillips, was "the sort to restore respect for a venerable and much abused profession." In the *Herald Tribune*, Lewis Gannett pointed out that the book's clarity and dramatic qualities obviously stemmed from the author's prior experience as a newspaperman. Moreover, wrote Gannett, the book contained a message for the future, one that set high standards for Kennedy himself. Gannett added the qualm that some of his colleagues will "regard it as highly irregular for a young Senator to write such a book as this." In Boston the City Council immediately passed an order requiring the School Committee to incorporate the book as an integral part of the history curriculum, while Councilor Gabriel F. Piemonte hailed the book as a "great lesson in democracy.". . .

The book itself was uncomplicated, written in clear, frequently dramatic language without any jargon; its style and theme made it perfectly suitable for the average reader. Its thrust was simple and its conclusion adhered to the best Whiggish concept of representative government. Those blessed with the responsibility for guiding the public's affairs must discharge their functions in the best interests of the commonwealth. Recalling that he had been advised upon entering the Congress that "the way to get along is to go along," Kennedy's theme addressed itself to the conflict inherent in a senator acting as the agent of the national need. One with better access to information and deliberation must necessarily find himself at variance with positions that are parochial and regional. The highest virtue of courage and patriotism, therefore, was the ability to resist local biases by placing expertise at the service of the national good. In each of the cases, according to the analysis presented by the book, the decision was initially unpopular. Kennedy himself pointed out that he did not necessarily agree with every particular historical stand; yet each one attested to a broader patriotism. Lucidly, the book enumerated an honor roll. The case studies constituted a judicious mixture of Republicans and Democrats. Their common denominator stressed the abandonment of "narrow" party interests for the greater good. . . .

In many ways, *Profiles* was a remarkable achievement from one currently holding legislative office. Perhaps, some have suggested, Kennedy was driven to expiate his guilt over the McCarthy affair. [Pleading illness, Kennedy had failed to register a vote on the censure of Senator Joseph R. McCarthy, a personal friend who was highly popular in Massachusetts.] Although willing to credit him with its authorship, few have assumed, as the preface more than hinted, that he lacked substantial assistance. James MacGregor Burns expressed this feeling by saying that "I think Sorensen or whoever was helping him, gave him more help on the book than you or I could help to get if we were doing one." One could properly inquire about what was unusual in modern American politics for a public figure, busily preoccupied with the demands of his office, to employ a capable staff that, using his name, could draft letters to editors for publication and even prepare correspondence, books, and articles under his byline.

The *Profiles* case was, however, exceptional—the difference between utilizing the prerequisites of office to expedite responsibilities and the manufacturing of a talent to create the image of a young senator distinctively different from conventional politicians and who, while denying that it was principally the work of others, would accept a Pulitzer prize. Enough personal recognition came his way to make it a major political coup. But it was as deceptive as installing a Chevrolet engine in a Cadillac.

The evidence is now available, perhaps as detailed as will ever be known. Relevant handwritten drafts, typescripts, and recorded tapes have been deposited with the Kennedy Library, all designed to validate his claims to authorship, as had previously been presented to private skeptics. Such material can also be augmented by those who were intimately associated with the project, who can provide corroborating details of how it was put together. Nothing in all this rejects the truth of Jack Kennedy's involvement: from start to finish, the responsibility was clearly his. . . .

Nevertheless, neither the chronology of Jack Kennedy's life in 1954 and 1955 nor the materials accumulated in the preparation of the book even come close to supporting the contention that Jack could have been or was its major author. Those were years when, in addition to being in the Senate, Kennedy underwent two major spinal operations and was hospitalized for three additional brief periods. He was also frequently absent on appearances throughout the country in an effort to further his credentials and visibility as a Democratic leader. It was also the period when he made an extensive European tour, from August to October of 1955.

The files do show notes in Kennedy's handwriting. Written on letter-size canary looseleaf paper, they contitute scrawls in his familiar tiny, slanted, almost indecipherable hand, much of the work probably done while on his back. They indicate very rough passages without paragraphing, without any shape, largely ideas jotted down as possible sections, obviously necessitating editing. That portion of the handwritten material, the pages cited by a seemingly endless crew of witnesses ready to testify that they actually watched him write, almost as though he were an author on display at work in a glass booth, in no way resembles the final product. Much of the writing contains notes from secondary sources that were mixed together with the original, creative passages. Almost all of the actual manuscript material rests in eight folders of Box 35 in the Kennedy Library. . . .

There is no evidence of a Kennedy draft for the overwhelming bulk of the book; and there is evidence for concluding that much of what he did draft was simply not included in the final version. The inescapable impression is that Kennedy's own interest, other than the question of representing one's conscience rather than merely reflecting constituent desires, largely related to John Quincy Adams, and he bogged down in that area, completely out of proportion to the needs of the book. Those who took over the project, headed by Sorensen, rescued him and helped fill out the material.

If the handwritten evidence is scant, dictation could have justified his claim to authorship. The existing tapes, however, duplicate the pattern of the nearly illegible scrawls on those canary sheets. His speech was characteristically rapid (especially during that stage of his life), the voice clipped, producing an almost indecipherable staccato effect, which must have been quite a chore for the typists. Still, the typescripts contained in the folders faithfully record his words, so it is possible to follow the text while hearing his voice, which often sounds distorted from either the aging of the tapes, the fact that he was under sedation, or the need to rest on his back. The overall effect, as in the handwritten sections, is that of disorganized, somewhat incoherent, melange from secondary sources, interspersed with quotes together with instructions for punctuation and style, and random observations. Many passages were read from Margaret Coit's biography of Calhoun. There was no attempt at creating a lucid narrative or structure. Obviously, it was data being transmitted for associates. The tapes also reveal that new recordings were made on top of the old, so that the existing reels do not represent the full extent of the dictation. If the Kennedy Library collection is designed to prove his authorship, it fails to pass inspection. About all the material does demonstrate is Jack's close association with its conception and completion.

For all the practical reasons, however—limitations of time, health, and appropriate talent—the senator served principally as an overseer or, more charitably, as a sponsor and editor, one whose final approval was as important for its publication as for its birth. At the working level, research, tentative drafts, and organizational planning were left to committee labor, with such talents as Professor [Jules] Davids making key contributions. But the burdens of time and literary craftmanship were clearly Sorensen's, and he gave the book both the drama and flow that made for readability.

Part Two

THE CAMPAIGNER

Chapter 6 THE FIRST CAMPAIGN

KENNETH P. O'DONNELL (1924–1977) and
DAVID F. POWERS (b. 1911) were two of
Kennedy's closest friends. Both were active in
Massachusetts politics and both were near the
President throughout the Thousand Days. Here
they describe the candidate's first campaign.
Does the selection reveal anything new about
Kennedy?

Dave Powers, with his precise memory for dates, names and figures, remembers that it was on the evening of January 21, 1946, that Jack Kennedy climbed the three flights of stairs to the top floor of the three-decker at 88 Ferrin Street in Charlestown and knocked on the front door. Fifteen years later, when they were swimming together in the pool at the White House, the President said to Dave, "If I had gotten tired that night when I reached the second floor, I never would have met you." Dave knew that the caller knocking on the front door of the cold-water flat must be a stranger. Three-decker families congregate in the kitchen, especially in the wintertime, to be close to the warmth of the kitchen stove, and their friends come up the back stairs to the kitchen door. Dave had just been discharged from the Army Air Force, after serving as a sergeant in China. He was living at the Ferrin Street apartment with his widowed older sister and her eight children. Like many newly discharged veterans that winter, Dave was at loose ends, drawing twenty dollars a week from the 52–20 Club, as the benefit payment for unemployed veterans was called, and helping to support his sister's family from his wartime savings.

"There was only a twenty-watt light bulb in the front hallway, and I could barely make out this tall and thin, handsome young fellow standing there alone in the semidarkness," Dave said, recalling the scene years later. "He stuck out his hand and said, 'My name is Jack Kennedy. I'm a candidate for Congress.' I said, 'Well, come on in.' While we were walking back toward the kitchen, where we could sit down and talk—my sister was listening to the radio in the parlor and the kids were in bed—he said that Bill Sutton had suggested me as somebody who might be able to help him in Charlestown. I said, 'Gosh, if I help anyone, it should be John Cotter.' I could see that didn't discourage him. He seemed rather ill at ease and shy, but I think the word to describe him that night, and I have used it often, is to say that he seemed aggressively shy. He knew what he wanted and he wouldn't give up. We talked for about twenty minutes about the people in the district and their needs. He had then that way of talking to you, asking you questions, and listening to you attentively that made you feel as though you were important—the only person in the world who mattered to him at the moment. He was really curious about finding out your ideas and your opinions. I heard a lot of people say that he impressed them that way later on when he was a Senator and when he was the President, but he was that way with me that first night we met in our kitchen back in 1946. I remember saying to him that the people in Charlestown were only looking for a decent place to live, an opportunity to give their children an education, and knowing where their next buck was coming from. He took that in as if he was trying to memorize it. He said, 'You know, that sounds about right.' "

When Jack was leaving, he mentioned casually that he was planning to attend a meeting of a group of Gold Star Mothers two days later at the American Legion hall in Charlestown. He asked if Dave would go to the meeting with him.

"I said I'd be glad to go with him to the meeting," Dave said later. "Here I had just told him that I was with John Cotter, but he was asking me to help him out and I was agreeing to it. I said to myself, 'Oh, well, I won't be doing Cotter any harm just going to this meeting with him.' So I made a date to meet him at his room in the Bellevue. I couldn't say no to him."

The meeting of the Gold Star Mothers was an afternoon party. Arriving at the Bellevue, Dave found Kennedy with a group of newly enlisted workers, all of them recently discharged veterans like himself, including Sutton and Eddie McLaughlin, who had served in the same PT-boat squadron with Jack and later became lieutenant governor in Massachusetts. Sutton said, "Do you want some of us to go with you?" Jack said quickly, "No, just Dave and I." This was one of his first political appearances—he did not announce his candidacy until two months later—but he was already instinctively setting the style of unpretentious restraint that was to set him apart from the old familiar type of flashy hat-waving politician. Then, as later, he disliked the thought of arriving at a speaking engagement in a big limousine, surrounded by an entourage of applause-leading lieutenants. Jack and Dave went to Charlestown that day on the subway. Dave noticed with surprise that Jack, unlike every politician that Dave had ever seen, was not wearing a hat. All during the months of campaigning that followed, Joe Kane continually urged Jack to wear a hat and Jack went bareheaded, ignoring Kane's complaint that his uncovered shock of boyishly tousled hair made him look as youthful as a high school student. Dave glanced at Jack's hair as the train came out of the subway and climbed the elevated tracks across the bridge to Charlestown, and said to himself. "This guy looks awfully young to be running for Congress." From the windows of the train on the high elevated structure above the Navy Yard and the old masts of the *Constitution*, Dave pointed out the wide view of the Congressional district—the Bunker Hill Monument ahead of them, Somerville and Cambridge in the distance at the left, and behind them the North End and East Boston. "And those are the kind of people you'll represent," Dave said, pointing below at the longshoremen and freight handlers working on the docks. Jack nodded thoughtfully and said, "Those are the kind of people I want to represent."

The young candidate's talk to the Gold Star Mothers at the American Legion hall was short and earnest. He spoke for ten minutes on the sacrifices of war and the need to keep the world at peace. Then he paused, looked at the women and said to them hesitantly, "I think I know how all you mothers feel because my mother is a gold star mother, too." All of the women in room stood up and hurried to the platform, crowding around Jack, shaking his hand and talking to him excitedly, smiling and wishing him good luck. "I had been to lot of political talks in Charlestown, but I never saw a reaction like this one." Dave said. "I heard those women saying to each other, 'Isn't he a wonderful boy, he reminds me so much of my own John, or my Bob.' They all had stars in their eyes. It took him a half hour to pull himself away from them. They didn't want to him to leave. I said to myself, I don't know what this guy's got. He's no great orator and he doesn't say much, but they certainly go crazy over him."

When Jack finally managed to make his way out of the hall, he turned to Dave and said to him, "How do you think I did?"

"How do I think you did?" Dave said. "You were terrific. I've never seen such a reaction from a crowd of people in my whole life."

"Then do you think you'll be with me?" Jack asked. "I'm already with you," Dave said. "I've already started working for you." They shook hands. Recalling that handshake recently, Dave, always the sentimental Irishman, added sadly, "And I stayed with him from that day until November 22, 1963, when I was riding in the car behind him in Dallas." . . . .

Slowly but surely as he declared his candidacy and the campaign got underway, Jack deftly moved his father's old political cigar-smoking friends into the background and replaced them with new young faces. Red Fay, his fellow PT-boat officer in the Pacific, was summoned from San Francisco and stayed for two months at the Bellevue until a terse letter from his father warned him that he had better get back to his job in the family's construction business. Torbert Macdonald, Jack's Harvard roommate, worked in Cambridge and in Somerville, where Ted Reardon, Young Joe Kennedy's college roommate, was in charge of the local headquarters. LeMoyne Billings, Jack's roommate at Choate School, was called to help out in the Cambridge office for a week or two, and ended up working there for the whole primary and election campaign, postponing until the next year his plan to do graduate work at the Harvard Business School. Bobby Kennedy, a youngster just out of the service as an enlisted man in the Navy, pitched in and worked hard for three months knocking on doors in East Cambridge, the most anti-Kennedy section of the district. His sister, Eunice, worked in the Boston headquarters. . . .

From the start of the campaign, Kennedy showed the incredible stamina and zest for hard work that was to set him apart in later years from other politicians. He would spend one whole a day a week in each of the district's community areas—one day in Cambridge, other days in Charlestown, Somerville, Brighton, East Boston, and the wards in downtown Boston—starting early in the morning, shaking hands at factory gates and on the waterfront docks, walking throughout the day shaking hands in shopping districts and visiting homes on residential streets, and ending up a night at local house parties and political meetings and rallies. Dave Powers' description of a typical day of campaigning in Charlestown, which was duplicated the next day and the day after that in other parts of the district:

"I would get him out of bed at the Bellevue Hotel around six-thirty in the morning and we'd rush over the bridge to Charlestown. He would stand outside the Charlestown Navy Yard from seven to eight, shaking thousands of workmen's hands as they went in to their jobs. By a quarter past eight, most of them were inside the yard and we would stop for breakfast. At nine o'clock we began a street tour, walking up Bunker Hill Street knocking on every door in that three-decker neighborhood. Most politicians are inclined to be lazy about campaigning. They go to rallies and meetings and dinners and luncheons, but they don't knock on people's doors. The housewives were startled to see Jack Kennedy standing on their porches because most of them had never seen a politician that closely before. He was the first one who took the trouble to come to them. He would talk to the Dohertys on the first floor, to the O'Briens on the second floor and the Murphys on the third floor.

"Those Irish mothers loved him. I could picture them, telling their sons that night that Jack Kennedy was there today and the family should vote for him. In an Irish home, the mother's word is law. The son doesn't argue with his mother.

"We'd stop for lunch—a frappe and a hamburger. A frappe is Boston for a milk shake with the ice cream beaten up in it. In the afternoon, we'd hit the barber shops, the neighborhood candy or variety stores and the taverns, the fire stations and the police stations. At four o'clock, back at the Navy Yard, catching the workers coming out of a different gate from the one where we worked that morning. They had three gates for their ten thousand workers. Then to the Bellevue for a shower and a change of clothes.

"In the evening there would be a rally or a political forum with all the candidates invited, and the house parties. We would arrange with young girls, school teachers or telephone operators or nurses, to invite their friends to a party at their house to meet Jack. The parties would range from small ones, with about fifteen people, to big ones that might take up two or three floors of a three-decker house. A wonderful girl named Ronnie Murphy gave a party at her house at 296 Bunker Hill Street one night where they must have had seventy people. Jack would go to three or four house parties in a night, one around seven-thirty and the later ones at eight or nine or nine-thirty.

"These people who met Jack at the house parties would turn out to be his workers. The next night they would be at our headquarters on Main Street, addressing envelopes or calling people on the telephone. We did a lot of work on getting young veterans just out of the service to register. Boys were coming home, just turning twenty-one, and we knew that with Jack Kennedy's great record in the war they would vote for him. The other guys who were working for Jack in other parts of the district— Teddy Reardon in Somerville, John Droney in Cambridge, Billy Kelly in East Boston, Tom Broderick in Brighton, Billy DeMarco in the North End—they would call me and say, "We heard you had fifty people working in your place last night. Where do you get them?' I would say, "Well, they meet Jack at the house parties and they become very enthusiastic.' "

The success of the house parties led to the famous Kennedy teas, formal receptions for women only, which later played an effective role in the statewide campaign for the Senate against Henry Cabot Lodge in 1952. Engraved invitations were sent to every woman on the locality's voting list, asking her to meet the candidate and his parents. For older women, the chance to get a close look at Rose Kennedy and the former Ambassador to the Court of Saint James's, the most celebrated couple to emerge from their generation of Boston Irish Catholics, was irresistible. Younger unmarried girls were thrilled to shake hands with Jack. As Patsy Mulkern, Joe Kane's precinct worker in Boston, observed at the time, "Before the teas, the hairdressers were working overtime and the dressmakers were taking dresses in and letting dresses out. Every girl in the district was dreaming and hoping that maybe lightning would strike." When the teas were first suggested, John Droney and others were against the idea, arguing that it seemed too effeminate in such a tough district.

"I was dead wrong," Droney says. "More than a thousand women turned out for the first tea at the Hotel Commander in Cambridge. They filed across the ballroom and passed along the reception line, each one shaking hands with Jack and his mother and father. I heard several of the women telling Jack that he would be President of the United States some day. An old Cambridge politician who was with me looked at the turnout and said, 'This kid will walk in.' I remember watching one elderly lady who marched up to the head of the receiving line, instead of waiting for her turn, and somebody took her by the arm to lead her away. Jack saw her, and excused himself from the people he was talking with and followed her across the ballroom floor, shook hands with her, asked who she was, and thanked her for coming. The old lady walked over to the table where they were serving tea and everybody could see that she was on cloud nine. The little scene made a nice impression on everybody there. In a situation like that you could count on Jack to do the right thing." . . . .

The grand climax of the Kennedy campaign was the appearance of the candidate and his followers in the annual Bunker Hill Day parade in Charlestown. Bunker Hill Day, the June seventeenth anniversary celebration of the Battle of Bunker Hill—the day before that year's primary voting—is a big holiday with fireworks in Boston, and its parade on Bunker Hill Street in Charlestown is an event among the Boston Irish rivaled only by the Saint Patrick's Day parade in South Boston. Dave Powers and his workers had placed Kennedy banners on every other house along the parade route. The Kennedy contingent marched as representatives of the Lieutenant Joseph P. Kennedy, Jr., Post 5880 of the Veterans of Foreign Wars, which Jack and his veteran friends had recently organized. Jack led the group, hatless in a dark flannel suit, with all of his youthful followers in white shirts. "People to this day tell me there were a thousand of us with Jack Kennedy in that parade," Dave Powers says. "Actually there were one hundred twenty-eight of us, but we marched only three abreast, stretching out the formation as long as we could. Up in front, Bill Sutton and Frank Dobie carried a big sign, 'John F. Kennedy for Congress,' about twenty feet wide and five feet high. People were running out into the street, shaking hands with him. I said to him, 'It's all over now.' But that last night, after the parade, he was still working. He went all over Charlestown, to the American Legion's open house, to the big dance at the Armory."

In the next day's primary, Kennedy led the field of ten candidates on the Democratic ballot with 42 percent of the total votes, 22,183 against Neville's 11,341 and Cotter's 6,671. As he expected, Kennedy was defeated by Neville in Cambridge by a slim margin of some 1,5000 votes and in Charlestown he was 337 votes behind Cotter, but he ran far ahead of both Neville and Cotter throughout the rest of the Congressional district. The other seven candidates trailed far behind. That night at the victory celebration in the Kennedy headquarters in Boston, Grandfather Fitzgerald climbed up on a table and sang "Sweet Adeline."

The next day Jack went to Cape Cod for some swimming and sailing. The election in November in that Democratic Congressional district was a mere formality. Kennedy buried the Republican candidate, Lester Bowen, with 69,000 votes to Bowen's 26,000, despite the fact that the Republicans swept Massachuetts that year. In his district, Kennedy received 13,000 votes more than the well-known Democratic governor, Maurice Tobin, who lost to the Republican Robert Bradford in his bid for reelection. The grandson of John F. Fitzgerald and Patrick J. Kennedy, soon to become the most successful Irish American politician of them all, was on his way to Washington.

Chapter 7 THE FIRST SENATE RACE

RICHARD J. WHALEN (b. 1935) is a Washington author, editor, and political consultant. His impressive *The Founding Father* gave us our first clear view of Joseph P. Kennedy. Here Whalen describes JFK's 1952 Senate race and the role played by the elder Kennedy. What were the three most important ingredients in the election victory?

As early as 1949, Jack Kennedy, though scarcely more than a freshman congressman, began running hard for higher office. It had taken only one term in the House for him to become bored with the tortoiselike pace of the seniority system. Restless and impatient, he found the satisfactions of the settled legislative life distinctly inferior to the excitement of capturing higher rank. What office he wanted, when he would seek it, and who his opponent would be—these questions were left to be decided by future opportunity.

Each Thursday evening, he flew from Washington to Boston, was met at the airport by his office manager, Frank Morissey, and set off in a chauffeur-driven car for a long weekend of speech-making across the state. On the following Monday evening, the undeclared candidate caught a plane back to the capital and resumed his congressional

From *The Founding Father: The Story Of Joseph P. Kennedy* by Richard J. Whalen, copyright 1966. Reprinted by permission of William Morris Agency on behalf of the author.

duties for another three days. As a leading member of the "Tuesday-to-Thursday Club" of Eastern congressmen and a notable absentee, Jack found little time to distinguish himself in the House. But by early 1952, he had crisscrossed Massachusetts dozens of times, introducing the name of Kennedy to voters in almost all of the state's three hundred and fifty-one cities and towns.

When he embarked on this long preliminary campaign, he considered trying for the governship in 1950, when the Democratic incumbent, Paul Dever, came up for reelection. State issues and politics were uninviting, but the executive position would make an excellent springboard to national office. Gradually, however, Jack changed his mind and moved toward a direct leap to the Senate in 1952. The way was cleared when Governor Dever, the logical challenger to Republican Senator Henry Cabot Lodge, fearful of the latter's popularity, chose to stay in the governor's mansion. Thirty-four-year-old Congressman Kennedy promptly announced his candidacy.

Most of the Bay State's professional politicians regarded it as a foolhardy move, likely to end in humiliating defeat. Lodge himself was supremely confident, and passed a message to Joe Kennedy through a mutual friend. "Lodge was considered unbeatable," Kennedy later remembered. "Do you know what Lodge said? He told Arthur Krock to 'tell Joe not to waste his money on Jack because he can't win. I'm going to win by three hundred thousand votes.' "

On the strength of Lodge's past performance, his boast was not extravagant. Since his first Senate victory in 1936, he had soundly beaten three popular Irish politicians— Jim Curley, Joseph Casey, and David I. Walsh. To achieve such triumphs in heavily Irish Massachusetts, it was necessary for him to attract the votes of loyal Democrats. Their defection reflected the changing Irish attitude toward the once-hated Brahmins. The envy and enmity of the nineteenth century steadily had given way to sentimental admiration and emulation. The descendants of Irish servants consciously shaped the manners and outlook of the old ruling class, which kept its place on top even after its power waned. With the political emergence of late-arriving ethnic groups, such as the Italians, the Irish identified themselves with the Yankee remnant and made common cause against the newcomers. The deep-seated Irish awe of the great Yankee families both annoyed and impressed Joe Kennedy. "All I ever heard when I was growing up in Boston," he recalled, "was how Lodge's grandfather had helped to put the stained glass windows into the Gate of Heaven Church in South Boston and they were still talking about those same stained glass windows in 1952 . . . ."

In family councils, Joe Kennedy advised his son to take on Lodge, saying, "When you've beaten him, you've beaten the best. Why try for something less?" That confident remark would be widely quoted as typical of the Kennedy fighting spirit, but it disclosed only part of the truth about how Kennedy fought. He never committed himself and his resources to a quixotic battle. He fought to win, but only after being convinced there was a chance of winning. For a year and a half before the 1952 campaign, a pair of paid, full-time Kennedy advance men toured the state, sounding out opinions, wooing local politicians, lining up likely volunteer workers. In addition to their detailed reports, Kennedy carefully weighted the findings of private polls. "You wonder why we're taking on Lodge," he confided to a friend. "We've seen polls. He'll be easier to beat than Leverett Saltonstall." Only after his cool head had confirmed his heart's desire did Kennedy encourage his son to go ahead.

In their recollections of 1952, father and son differed on the role the elder Kennedy played in the campaign. As Jack remembered that summer and fall, his father had stayed on the sidelines at Hyannis Port. However, Joe Kennedy recalled that he had been in Boston—and so he had. Jack's attempt to minimize his father's contribution was part of his general defensiveness about how he had won, and why. As he said several years afterward, "People say, 'Kennedy bought the election. Kennedy could never have been elected if his father hadn't been a millionaire.' Well, it wasn't the Kennedy name and the Kennedy money that won that election. I beat Lodge because I hustled for three years. I worked for what I got."

Work he did. But whether or not he acknowledged it, the name and wealth bestowed on him by his father made victory possible. At the time, Joe Kennedy acted as though he was fully aware of this fact. "The father was the distinct boss in every way," said one who attended pre-campaign strategy meetings at the Kennedy home on Cape Cod in the spring of 1952. "He dominated everything, even told everyone where to sit. They [were] just children in that house."

It was evident to outsiders that Jack, in his father's presence, felt the need gently to assert his authority. Running down a list of assignments at an early planning session, the candidate facetiously delegated to his father the task of making all the money. "We concede you that role," he said.

As in 1946, Joe Kennedy went ahead in his usual fashion, asking no one's permission and sometimes acting without his son's knowledge. "The father was a tremendous factor in the campaign," said a Boston lawyer and campaign worker. "He remained out of public view. He didn't run things, but they happened according to his plans. He cast the die. . . ."

Quiet, mild-mannered Mark Dalton, who had managed Jack's previous campaigns for the House, loyally returned to his post. By 1952, Dalton's law practice had grown to the point where he no longer could afford the sacrifice of working as an unpaid volunteer, and so he agreed to take a salary. This new arrangement lasted just two weeks. "Dalton was at his desk, smoking a pipe, when Joe Kennedy breezed in," said one who witnessed the scene. "The old man spread all the books on the desk in front of him, studied them for about five minutes without saying a word, then he shoved his finger in Dalton's face and yelled: 'Dalton, you've spent ten thousand dollars of my money and you haven't accomplished a damn thing.' The next day Dalton was gone."

Money, as such, had nothing to do with Dalton's abrupt departure. Once again, Kennedy's retainer, John Ford, was serving as overseer of campaign finances, so Kennedy knew very well whom to blame if funds were misspent. His outburst may have been intended as a reminder to the hardworking Dalton that, having accepted a salary, he now became just another of Kennedy's employees.

Twenty-six-year-old Bobby Kennedy, fresh from the University of Virginia Law School, became campaign manager. "When Bobby came in," an insider said later, "we knew it was the old man taking over. What had Bobby done up to that time politically? Nothing. Not a damn thing and all of a sudden he was there as campaign manager, waving the banners." At the very least, the choice provided further proof, if any was needed, that Kennedys preferred to deal with Kennedys.

The inexperienced Bobby showed little deference toward older politicians. As much a stranger in Boston as his older brother had been, he knew almost none of the local powers. One very prominent Boston political figure paid a visit to the newly opened Kennedy headquarters and was astounded to discover that no one, not even the candidate's manager, recognized him. "You're asking me who I am?" he shouted. "You mean to say nobody here knows me? And you call this a political headquarters?" Annoyed, Bobby threw the caller out.

Some professionals found the young amateur insufferable. Governor Dever was running for reelection and his campaign was linked was Jack Kennedy's. One day, Bobby stormed into Dever's office and began to berate him for what he considered a mistake in strategy. Dever angrily cut him short and showed him the door. Then he telephoned the Ambassador: "I know you're an important man around here and all that, but I'm telling you this and I mean it. Keep that fresh kid of yours out of my sight from here on in. . . ."

Jack Kennedy's 1952 campaign wrote Ralph G. Martin and Ed Plaut in their book, *Front Runner, Dark Horse*, "was the most methodical, the most scientific, the most thoroughly detailed, the most intricate, the most disciplined and smoothly working statewide campaign in Massachusetts history—and possibly anywhere else." Busy behind the scenes at the center of this enterprise, incessantly demanding perfection, was Joe Kennedy. "The Ambassador worked around the clock," said one of the speech-writers he brought to Boston. "He was always consulting people, getting reports, looking into problems. Should Jack go on TV with this issue? What kind of an ad should he run on something else? He'd call in experts, get opinions, have ideas worked up."

It was understood by all concerned that the candidate would make the final decisions, but the alternatives set before him usually were framed by his father's hand-picked "braintrust." When unmade decisions piled up, as often happened in those hectic days, there was no question about where to turn. "Sometimes you couldn't get anybody to make a decision," a worker recalled. "You'd have to call the old man. Then you'd get a decision."

The 1952 campaign, though broader and more complex, divided into essentially the same two sides as the race for the House six years earlier. The candidate, under the nominal managership of his brother and surrounded by a phalanx of energetic young men, carried the battle to the far corners of the state. Back in Boston, unseen but hard at work, were the specialists and professionals on the elder Kennedy's payroll. Those who slipped in and out of his suite at the Ritz-Carlton included Jim Landis; Lynn

Johnson, a lawyer from the Kennedy headquarters in Manhattan; John Harriman, on leave from his job as a financial writer on the *Boston Globe*, and Sargent Shriver, formerly on the staff of *Newsweek* and more recently a dollar-a-year man at the Department of Justice, where he had assisted Eunice Kennedy in a study of juvenile delinquency. Many others also were active, coming forward as their talents were needed.

At work throughout Massachusetts were two hundred and eighty-six Kennedy "secretaries," backed by an army of more than twenty thousand volunteers. Jack Kennedy had had no opposition in the Democratic primary, thus losing an opportunity to test-run his newly built machine, but he did require twenty-five hundred signatures on his nomination papers. Someone suggested the workers should be encouraged to get as many signatures as possible. They collected more than a hundred times the number required—a record 262,324. A measure of the money spent on the campaign was the fact that each person who signed received a thank-you letter.

The magnitude of the Kennedy publicity effort was staggering. Distributed across the state were nine hundred thousand copies of an eight-page tabloid featuring drawings of Lieutenant Kennedy rescuing his shipmates in the Pacific. On the facing page was a photograph of young Joe Kennedy whose fatal war mission was described under this headline. "John Fulfills Dream of Brother Joe Who Met Death in the Sky Over the English Channel." Inserted in each paper was a *Reader's Digest* reprint of John Hersey's article on the saga of PT-109, which originally had appeared in *The New Yorker*.

Still, the most impressive feature in this vast campaign—indeed, the Kennedy hallmark—was painstaking attention to small detail. In June, Boston's Mayor John B. Hynes appeared at a rally at the Copley-Plaza launching Jack Kennedy campaign. "The speeches were televised," Hynes later recalled, "and for the first time I saw a Teleprompter. In fact, there were two of them, and I wondered why." When one broke down and the other kept the show running smoothly, Hynes realized he was in the company of perfectionists.

This efficient organization tried, with only limited success, to manufacture campaign issues. A major Kennedy theme was to blame Lodge for the state's industrial decline and unemployment, all the while ignoring Governor Dever's campaign claim that the economy had flourished under his leadership. Empty sloganeering was the order of the day. "KENNEDY WILL DO MORE FOR MASSACHUSETTS," proclaimed the challenger's posters. To which the Lodge forces brightly replied: "LODGE HAS DONE—AND WILL DO—THE MOST FOR MASSACHUSETTS."

Much more effective was the decision of the Kennedy strategists to outflank Lodge on both the left and right, a boldly opportunistic maneuver that was feasible only because Jack Kennedy's own position was highly ambiguous. On the one hand, he criticized Lodge as a moss-back conservative, pointing to his own down-the-line support of the Truman administration's "Fair Deal" domestic program. On the other hand, Kennedy attacked his opponent for giving too much support to the Truman administration's foreign policy. Lodge was accused of weakneed bipartisanship, while Kennedy, in the words of a study prepared by his staff, "has been an outspoken critic of many elements of the Administration's Foreign Policy." In this respect, the study continued, "he has been much closer to the position of [Senator Robert A.] Taft than has Lodge. . . ."

This plea for the votes of conservative Republicans was urged by Joe Kennedy, who shrewdly guessed that the followers of Senator Taft in Massachusetts might well have a decisive influence on the Kennedy-Lodge contest. . . .

Long after the campaign, a worker vividly remembered Joe Kennedy's "terrible anguish" at the possibility that the shadow of his rumored anti-Semitism would fall across his son's path. As it turned out, the steady defection of leading Jews to Kennedy caused panic among some of Lodge's supporters, and led them into a move that backfired. They flooded Jewish neighborhoods with a flier declaring, "GERMAN DOCUMENTS ALLEGE KENNEDY HELD ANTI-SEMITIC VIEWS." The flier was based on a three-year-old newspaper story reporting the State Department's publication of the dispatches of German Ambassador Dirksen, in which he had attributed pro-Nazi and anti-Semitic statements to Ambassador Kennedy. Quickly Kennedy's workers put out an answering leaflet: "SHAME ON YOU MR. LODGE! Lodge Endorses McCarthy in Wisconsin and Lodge Supporters Use McCarthy Tactics Here. . . ."

The indirect attack on "McCarthyism," carefully addressed to an especially receptive group of voters, marked the only time the Kennedy campaign publicly mentioned the name of Senator Joseph R. McCarthy, the explosively controversial anti-Communist crusader. In order to minimize the use of McCarthy's name, the Kennedy people hired the same men who had circulated the Lodge flier to circulate theirs to the same homes only. The determined effort to pretend that McCarthy did not exist, motivated by fear of his enthusiastic following in Massachusetts, was not without a certain irony.

For McCarthy was a good friend of the Kennedy family, and particularly of the Ambassador. "In case there is any question in your mind," Joe Kennedy told an interviewer in 1961, "I liked Joe McCarthy. I always liked him. I would see him when I went down to Washington, and when he was visiting in Palm Beach he'd come around to my house for a drink. I invited him to Cape Cod." At Hyannis Port one Fourth of July, McCarthy, playing shortstop for the Kennedy team ("the Barefoot Boys") in the traditional softball game on the lawn, committed four errors and was retired summarily to the porch. Another time, the Ambassador remembered, "he went out on my boat . . . . and he almost drowned swimming behind it, but he never complained."

It was McCarthy's unfailing good nature that commended him to Kennedy. "He was always pleasant; he was never a crab. If somebody was against him, he never tried to cut his heart out. He never said that anybody was a stinker. He was a pleasant fellow."

When McCarthy began his one-man war on communism, Kennedy later said, "I thought he'd be a sensation. He was smart. But he went off the deep end." In recalling his friend's sad end, the interviewer noted, Kennedy's voice quavered and his eyes clouded.

But in 1952, Kennedy saw clearly enough that McCarthy, if he came to Massachusetts on behalf of Lodge, could destroy his son's chances. According to Westbrook Pegler, Kennedy took steps to keep the Senator away. That year McCarthy had undergone a serious operation, was almost broke, and faced a tough primary fight in Wisconsin. As Kennedy later remembered the incident, "I gave Joe McCarthy a small contribution, sure, but it was only a couple of thousand dollars, and I didn't give it to him to keep him out of Massachusetts, I gave it to him because a mutual friend of ours, Westbrook Pegler, asked me to give it to him . . . ."

Wrote Pegler in 1960: "My statement is that I did not ask Kennedy to give any money to McCarthy. We were discussing McCarthy's illness and his busted condition. . . . And Joe Kennedy volunteered to send McCarthy $3,000 in currency and asked me to transmit the money itself. I took counsel of a wiser head who warned me not to touch the money or have anything to do with the deal. Therefore I kept hands off and I was told later in New York that an intimate friend of the Kennedys, and an old friend of mine, arranged to deliver the money to McCarthy. But I did not 'ask' Joe Kennedy to do anything for McCarthy, although by this time he may believe my mention of Joe's financial problem amounted to a request. . . .

"I did not then suspect that Joe's motive in contributing to McCarthy was to keep McCarthy out of Massachusetts. But soon afterward a wise and cynical head in New York who had known Joe Kennedy of old said, 'Joe will be around to collect from McCarthy.' He was dead right. Those Kennedys are cold-blooded and long-headed but it takes experience and disillusionment to learn them." In the fall of 1952, concluded Pegler, "Joe Kennedy asked me to persuade McCarthy to keep out of Massachusetts. So my New York sage had been right. This was to be the payoff. Still, I didn't mind. I told McCarthy to let Lodge croak and foolishly ventured that Jack Kennedy, though a Democrat, was at heart a fine American. . . . Joe Kennedy later admitted freely to me that his [McCarthy's] abstention from the fight in Massachusetts had been helpful—possibly he said decisive in young Jack's victory over Lodge."

McCarthy, for one reason or another, did not come to Massachusetts, but the question of "McCarthyism," and the candidate's attitude toward it, came up inside the Kennedy organization. When it did, Joe Kennedy put his foot down—hard.

To help him outflank Lodge on the liberal side, Jack Kennedy had recruited Gardner (Pat) Jackson, a Bostonian whose championship of Liberal causes dated back to the trial of Sacco and Vanzetti. An unreconstructed New Dealer who had broken with Henry Wallace and John L. Lewis because of their imperfect devotion to liberalism, Jackson agreed to work for Jack in spite of misgivings about his father. ("Did Jack's father ask me to help?" said Jackson later. "He did NOT!") After much arguing and pleading, he was able to mobilize behind Kennedy the initially skeptical labor unions and the Americans for Democratic Action. Having sold his candidate as a liberal, Jackson, not surprisingly, wished him to behave like one. The cause then closest to his heart was the fight against "McCarthyism," and he tried to persuade Jack to take a stand. Jackson prepared a carefully worded newspaper advertisement, which quoted from the statement by ninety-nine members of the Notre Dame faculty. The headline read: "COMMUNISM AND McCARTHY: BOTH WRONG." Jack finally consented to sign it, provided Congressman McCormack would co-sign it. McCormick agreed. Triumphantly, Jackson set out the next morning, a copy of the ad in his pocket, for the small apartment Jack had rented at 122 Bowdoin Street.

"The place was a hubbub of activity," Jackson later recalled. "Jack had his coat on and went dashing out just as I arrived." The reason for the unusually early morning activity was apparent: Joe Kennedy was paying a call. Seated with him at a card table in the center of the room were three of his son's speech-writers: Jim Landis, John Harriman, and Joe Healy. Before Jack left, he asked that Jackson read the ad he had prepared.

". . . . I hadn't gone two sentences when Joe [Kennedy] jumped to his feet with such force that he tilted the table against the others," he remembered. For a moment, it seemed as though the enraged Kennedy would physically attack Jackson. Instead, as the others looked on in embarrassed silence, he violently berated him. "You're trying to ruin Jack. You and your sheeny friends are trying to ruin my son's career," shouted Kennedy, who said that he liked McCarthy and had contributed to his campaign. Again and again he accused the liberals and union people of hurting his son. "I can't estimate how long he poured it out on me," recalled Jackson. "It was just a stream of stuff—always referring to 'you and your sheeny friends.' " His fury spent, Kennedy stalked out.

The McCarthy ad, of course, was dead. Next morning, Jackson and the candidate were alone in the apartment.

"I hear you really had it yesterday, didn't you?" said Jack, trying to soothe the older man.

"How do you explain your father?" Jackson asked.

"I guess there isn't a motive in it which I think you'd respect," said Jack, "except love of family." He paused for a moment, then added, "And more often than not, I think that's just pride. . . ."

Through the campaign, those around Jack often doubted his ability to bear up physically. His spinal operation had failed to heal properly, and he was in almost constant pain. On his trip with Bobby and Pat in 1951, he had become seriously ill, and was flown to a military hospital on Okinawa with a temperature above 106 degrees. ("They didn't think he would live," Bobby later recalled.) Midway through the campaign, Jack was unable to move with crutches, but he refused to admit his body's weakness. "He hated to appear in public on his crutches," said a friend who traveled with him. "When we came to the door of a hall where he was to make a speech, he'd hand the crutches to one of us and throw his shoulders back and march down the aisle as straight as a West Point cadet. How he did it, I'll never know."

An unfailing source of strength was the support he received from his family. "Each Kennedy," a reporter once observed, "takes pride in the achievements of the others. Each, instinctively, had rather win the approval of the family than of outsiders. And when an outsider threatens to thwart the ambitions of any of them, the whole family forms a close-packed ring, horns lowered, like a herd of bison beset by wolves." Accused of being self-centered, the Kennedys also were respected for their remarkable solidarity. "I don't worry about Jack Kennedy. I don't worry about Kennedy's money," moaned a Lodge supporter. "It's that family of his . . . . they're all over the state."

Lodge, who had been busy working for Eisenhower, belatedly recognized his peril and came hurrying back to Massachusetts two months before the election. By that time, members of the Kennedy family had shaken the hands of some two million voters. During the campaign, no fewer than thirty-three formal receptions were given, attended by an estimated seventy-five thousand persons, almost all of them women. Rose Kennedy came directly from Paris for the first reception, arriving from New York's Idlewild Airport in a chauffeured limousine. Jack's standard appeal was brief and boyish. "In the first place," he told the ladies, "for some strange reason, there are more women than men in Massachusetts, and they live longer. Secondly, my grandfather, the late John F. Fitzgerald, ran for the United States Senate thirty-six years ago against my opponent's grandfather, Henry Cabot Lodge, and he lost by only thirty thousand votes in an election where women were not allowed to vote. I hope that by impressing the female electorate that I can more than take up the slack."

The handsome young congressman made a dazzling impression: an estimated 80 percent of his volunteer workers were signed up at the receptions. "What is there about Jack Kennedy," a Republican visitor was heard to ask, "that makes every Catholic girl in Boston between eighteen and twenty-eight think it's a holy crusade to get him elected?" Women of all ages were awed by the family's trappings of wealth and power. A veteran newspapermen cynically remarked that "it was all they could do to keep those old gals who came to the affairs from curtsying. They had every tendency to drop to one knee."

The candidate's brothers and sisters rang doorbells, made speeches, attended house parties, and twice appeared on a family television program, "Coffee with the Kennedys." But the star of the family campaign troupe turned out to be Rose. Jack's organization was weakest in Boston, and his father summoned a seasoned professional, State Senator John Powers, to take the situation in hand.

"I told him," said Powers, "that he was right about Boston. I said to him, 'Joe, the fight's falling off and it needs something to pick it up. I asked him for permission to use Mrs. Kennedy. He answered, 'But Johnny, she's a grandmother!

"That's all right,' I told him, 'she's a Gold Star mother, the mother of a war hero and a congressman, the wife of an Ambassador, the daughter of a mayor and a congressman, the daughter-in-law of a state senator and representative and she's beautiful and she's a Kennedy. Let me have her.' And he thought it over and finally said, 'Well, take it slow with her.' "

Joe's concern was misplaced. The daughter of "Honey Fitz" knew exactly what to say and do, no matter what the audience. Before a group of Italian women in Boston's North End, she appeared as a girl who had grown up in the neighborhood, the mother of nine children. She greeted her audience with a few words of Italian, and then showed the card index file she had used to keep track of her children's illnesses, vaccinations, and dental work. She might wear a simple black dress and a single strand of pearls. In her limousine en route to a gathering of Chestnut hill matrons, she would don jewelry and a mink stole, as befit the Ambassador's lady. After speaking a few minutes about her son, Rose would say, "Now, let me tell you about the new dresses I saw in Paris last month."

On election night, the workers at Kennedy headquarters watched tensely as a year and a half of planning, and more than six months of unremitting effort, were put to the test. Hour by hour, the returns swayed back and forth. By early morning, it was clear that Eisenhower would sweep the state. Lodge might ride Ike's landslide to victory. But Jack Kennedy remained serene, never doubting that he would win. At six o'clock in the morning, Lodge conceded. The final returns showed that while Eisenhower was swamping Stevenson, and Dever was being narrowly defeated by Christian Herter for the governorship, Kennedy had pulled a stunning upset, defeating Lodge by more than seventy thousand votes.

Had Joe Kennedy bought his son's election? Many would argue that he had. Estimates of the Kennedy spending ran up to a wildly improbable several million dollars. It was true that Kennedy had outspent Lodge by a substantial margin. The various Kennedy committees, operating independently of the Democratic party fund-raising groups, officially reported expenses of just under $350,000. The whole cost of the Kennedy campaign was probably well above half a million dollars, how much above, no one would ever know. Officially, Lodge reported expenses of only $59,000. In addition, he benefited heavily from the Republican party's record million-dollar spending for the state ticket.

"It was those damned tea parties," Lodge said afterward. In a sense, he was right. He had been defeated by a young patrician whose rise was shared vicariously by thousands of Irish-Americans. Where their grandfathers dreamed of awakening as Yankee overlords, now they might dream of becoming Kennedys. Into the family's victory, went money, hard work, and a long, unforgiving memory. Said Rose Fitzgerald Kennedy following the election: "At last, the Fitzgeralds have evened the score with the Lodges!"

Chapter 8 THE PRESIDENTIAL CONTEST

THEODORE H. WHITE (1915–86) became a Kennedy admirer during the Senator's presidential campaign. A liberal journalist and fellow Harvard graduate, White wrote a book length account of the 1960 campaign that became a classic. In this excerpt from *The Making Of The President, 1960*, White describes several reasons for Kennedy's popularity. Why did reporters especially enjoy being in the company of the Democratic candidate?

So, slowly, in the first ten days of his campaign, John F. Kennedy began to find both style and theme; and listening, as the reporters did, to the same five minute "all-purpose" speech six or eight times a day, hearing it change from state to state and city to city, they could see both the change in style and the development of theme that was to shape the Kennedy campaign and the election.

Kennedy began his first round taut and tense, his voice rapid and rushed, as if trying to make up for lost time; he appeared uncertain—or so it seemed to listeners—as to what was quite the proper manner and posture of a man who seeks the Presidency. Then, gradually, his little crossroads all-purpose speeches grew easier. Personal touches showed the change—like mention of the expected baby. Out of his sense of privacy, Kennedy had omitted mentioning his wife or her pregnant condition

From *The Making of the President, 1960* by Theodore H. White, copyright 1961. Reprinted by permission of Macmillan Publishing Company and Laurence Pollinger Limited.

in the early days of his campaign—and a tribute to the wife is rigidly required in American political orthodoxy. Then, one noon in the warm sun in the little park behind the gleaming color-splashed courthouse of Eugene, Oregon, he impulsively offered the courteous excuse that his wife was absent because she was "otherwise committed." A friendly ripple of laughter followed. The next morning, in northern California, he had changed it to "My wife has other responsibilities," and a warmer laugh followed. By afternoon the phrase had become a forthright "My wife is going to have a baby." In the San Joaquin valley the next day it was "My wife is going to have a boy in November." It had become a certified gag; and that afternoon in Los Angeles, it became a press-conference question that ended a tense interchange of questions on religion. "How do you know it's going to be a boy?" asked the questioner. "My wife told me," said Kennedy, and the conference ended with a laugh.

What was more important than the slow growth of ease was the development in the humble all-purpose speech of the grand theme that was to dominate and shape his campaign to the end: *America cannot stand still; her prestige fails in the world; this is a time of burdens and sacrifice; we must move.*

He began his first round with a loose collection of phrases and anecdotes that he jumbled into a pudding for the all-purpose speech: a collection of historical anecdotes, and then the standard phrases: "the importance of the Presidency"; "the world cannot exist half slave and half free"; "only the President can lead"; "farming is our number one domestic problem"; "automation can be a blessing or a curse"; "we must move"; "I ask your help."

Then, gradually, as applause told him where he had hit and indifference informed him where he talked beyond the audience, the pattern began to shape itself into a theme. It seemed to do so most clearly in a glorious two-day passage down the valleys of California, as his campaign train, full of politicians, soothed by wine, crowds and proximity to the great, rocked over the roadbed of the Southern Pacific.

The train had left Portland, Oregon, the previous evening, and the California interlude opened from its rear platform the next morning in Dunsmuir, California, a tiny hill station sunk in a glen of giant redwoods that rose as a silent audience above the little knot of people who had risen at six in the morning to look at a Presidentical candidate.

He spoke for three minutes from the platform, and his voice rang through the forest glade: ". . . . I thank you very much for coming down. This is an important campaign because it is an important country, and because all of us are anxious to see the United States move ahead. I ask your help in this campaign. . . ."

He spoke at Red Bluff an hour later and the sun was higher, but he was still in forest country.

"I campaign for the office of Presidency in a very difficult and dangerous time in the life of our country, and I do not do so promising that if I am elected all of the problems of California and the United States and the free world will be solved. . . . But we must recognize the close relationships between the vitality of our own domestic economy and our position around the world. If we stand still here at home, we stand still around the world. . . ."

At Richmond, California, by late afternoon, he was in gut-Democratic territory, and he was embroidering.

"If you think we can provide better schools for our children and more help for the older, if you think we can develop this state and the resources of the West, if you think it is possible to strengthen the image and prestige of the United States around the world, then come with us. If you are tired and don't want to move, then stay with the Republicans. But I think we are ready to move [Applause]. . . ."

. . . as the debates ended and the Kennedy campaign entered its third and last round, whoever traveled with the Democratic candidate became dazzled, then blinded, with the radiance of approaching victory. Warnings might come from rear-echelon headquarters, but for those who traveled the combat front with the combat element of John F. Kennedy, it seemed impossible there could be danger still. For in the six weeks since mid-September, this campaign, and the campaigners with it, had changed: decisions now came with snap and confidence; the machinery purred; the candidate's style seemed to top itself with each day's touring; and the response, there before one's eyes, overwhelmed judgment. . . .

The most interesting and precise of the decisions of this period, however, was one made by the candidate himself—particularly as it contrasted with the simultaneous Nixon decision on the same problem. This concerned the Martin Luther King affair— an episode that tangled conscience with the most delicate balancing of the Northern Negro-Southern white vote.

Martin Luther King is one of the genuine heroes of the tumultuous Negro struggle for authentic equality in American life; a luminous man, he speaks responsibly for the best there is in his community. On Wednesday, October 19th—at about the same time of day that John Kennedy and Richard Nixon were addressing the American Legion in Miami on the national defense—Martin Luther King was arrested with fifty-two other Negroes in Rich's Department Store in Atlanta for refusing to leave a table in its Magnolia Room restaurant. On the following Monday, all other "sit-ins" arrested in this episode were released; King along was held in jail and, worse, sentenced on a technicality to four months' hard labor and thereupon whisked away secretly to the State Penitentiary. This was no ordinary arrest—no Negro in America has more deservedly earned greater warmth and adoration from his fellow Negroes, North or South, than Martin Luther King; but no Negro menaces the traditional prerogatives of Southern whites more importantly. It was not beyond possibility that he would never emerge alive from the Reidsville (Georgia) State Prison, deep in "cracker" country, where he had been taken; nor did anyone believe more in the prospect of his lynching than his wife, then six months pregnant. Had King been lynched, the violence that would have resulted would have overmatched the violence later shown by the American Negro community over the lynching of Patrice Lumumba in Africa, in inverse proportion to the distance between Georgia and Katanga. The American Negro community girded; so did the Southern whites; during the previous few weeks, even before the arrest, no less than three Southern governors had informed Kennedy headquarters directly that if he intruded in Southern affairs to support or endorse Martin Luther King, then the South could be given up as lost to the Democratic ticket. Now Kennedy must choose. This was a crisis.

The crisis was instantly recognized by all concerned with the Kennedy campaign. On the night of Tuesday, October 25th, the suggestion for meeting it was born to one of those remarkably competent young men that the Kennedy organization had brought into politics to direct the Civil Rights Section of their campaign, a Notre Dame law profesor named Harris Wofford. Wofford's idea was as simple as it was human—that the candidate telephone directly to Mrs. King in Georgia to express his concern. Desperately Wofford tried to reach his own chief, Sargent Shriver, head of the Civil Rights Section of the Kennedy campaign, so that Shriver might break through to the candidate barnstorming somewhere in the Middle West. Early Wednesday morning, Wofford was able to locate Shriver, the gentlest and warmest of the Kennedy clan (he had married Eunice Kennedy, the candidate's favorite sister) in Chicago—and Shriver enthusiastically agreed. Moving fast, Shriver reached the candidate at O'Hare Inn at Chicago's International Airport as the latter was preparing to leave for a day of barnstorming in Michigan.

The candidate's reaction to Wofford's suggestion of participation was impulsive, direct and immediate. From his room at the Inn, without consulting anyone, he placed a long-distance telephone call to Mrs. Martin Luther King, assured her of his interest and concern in her suffering and, if necessary, his intervention.

Mrs. King, elated yet still upset, informed a few of her closest friends. Through channels of Negro leadership, the word swiftly sped north from Atlanta, and thus to the press, that Kennedy had intervened to protect the imprisoned Negro leader. And Bobby Kennedy, informed in the course of the day of the command decision, proceeded even further and the next morning telephoned a plea for King's release from New York to the Georgian judge who had set the sentence; on Thursday King was released from Reidsville prison on bail, pending appeal—safe and sound.

The entire episode received only casual notice from the generality of American citizens in the heat of the last three weeks of the Presidential campaign. But in the Negro community the Kennedy intervention rang like a carillon. The father of Martin Luther King, a Baptist minister himself, who had come out for Nixon a few weeks earlier on religious grounds, now switched. "Because this man," said the Reverend Mr. King, Senior, "was willing to wipe the tears from my daughter[-in-law]'s eyes, I've got a suitcase of votes, and I'm going to take them to Mr. Kennedy and dump them in his lap." Across the country scores of Negro leaders, deeply Protestant but even more deeply impressed by Kennedy's action, followed suit. And where command decision had been made, the Kennedy organization could by now follow through. Under Wofford's direction a million pamphlets describing the episode were printed across the country, half a million in Chicago alone, whence they were shipped by

Greyhound bus. On the Sunday before election, these pamphlets were distributed outside Negro Churches all across the country. One cannot identify in the narrowness of American voting of 1960 any one particular episode or decision as being more important than any other in the final tallies: yet when one reflects that Illinois was carried by only 9,000 votes and that 250,000 Negroes are estimated to have voted for Kennedy; that Michigan was carried by 67,000 votes and that an estimated 250,000 Negroes voted for Kennedy; that South Carolina was carried by 10,000 votes and that an estimated 40,000 Negroes there voted for Kennedy, the candidate's instinctive decision must be ranked among the most crucial of the last few weeks. . . .

Saturday, October 1st, at Hyannisport had been Kennedy's last day of rest. From then until election day, his hours grew longer, his sleep less frequent (in the last four days of the campaign, he averaged only four hours a night). Yet his voice grew stronger and slower. Earlier in the campaign, when he feared his voice might not last the weeks ahead, he had communicated with his staff on the plane by scrawling conversational answers on yellow pads as they talked with him. Now he wanted to stay up on the plane and talk—sometimes for hours, about all manners of things. It was as if second wind were coming to a long-distance runner; and, as his manner of delivery grew slower, his public language grew more elegant. His style, finally, began to capture even the newsmen who had heard all he had to say long before, but continued to listen, as one continues to return to a favorite movie.

Most of all, he seemed to be enjoying himself as the mobs stimulated adrenalin in his arteries; and the crispest edge of his enjoyment seemed to be the taunting of Nixon. This was supposed to be the all-out slash-and-hack last phase of the Nixon attack on Kennedy. But it was as if Nixon were wielding a club while Kennedy pinked him with a rapier. Kennedy particularly liked the phrase, borrowed from the Spanish bullfight ring, of *mano a mano*, or hand-to-hand combat; this was *mano a mano*, and he liked it. . . .

. . . the Kennedy crowds were spectacular. It was not the numbers that made them spectacular (Kennedy's top crowd in his Broadway parade in New York on October 19th probably came to no more than 1,250,000 a figure that could be matched by an Eisenhower peak in the Eisenhower campaigns) but their frenzied quality.

One remembers being in a Kennedy crowd and suddenly sensing far off on the edge of it a ripple of pressure beginning, and the ripple, which always started at that back, would grow like a wave, surging forward as it gathered strength, until it would squeeze the front rank of the crowd against the wooden barricade, and the barricade would begin to splinter; then the police would rush to reinforce the barricade, shove back, start a counterripple, and thousands of bodies would, helplessly but ecstatically, be locked in the rhythmic back-and-forth rocking. One remembers the groans and the moans; and a frowzy woman muttering hoarsely as if to herself, "Oh, Jack I love yuh, Jack, I love yuh, Jack—Jack, Jack, I love yuh"; or the harsh-faced woman peering over one's shoulder glowering, "You a newspaperman?—You better write nice things about him, or you watch out" (and she meant it). One remembers the crude signs—

hand-lettered, crayoned by school children, chalked on tarpaulin by workmen constructing new buildings, carried on staves by families (in the Bronx: "The home of the knishes thinks Jack is delicious" and "The home of the bagel thinks Big Jack is Able"). And the noise, and the clamor.

One remembers the motorcades and the people along the road—confetti pouring down at some stops until, when the convertible's door would open to release the candidate, the confetti would pour out like water from a tank. One remembers groups along the road waving, the women unbinding kerchiefs from their heads to wave; the grizzled workingmen and union men, too embarrassed to show emotion publicly, toughness written all over their hard faces, suddenly holding out their hands and waving at him after he had gone by—and the hand stretched out as in a Roman salute of farewell for full seconds after the candidate had passed, and then slowly dropping, of itself. One remembers the grabbers, bursting through police lines, trying to touch him or reach him, and the squeezers who grasped his hand and, to prove their affection, squeezed extra hard until, one day in Pennsylvania, even the candidate's calloused hand burst with blood.

One remembers, of course, the jumpers. The jumpers made their appearance shortly after the first TV debate when from a politician Kennedy had become, in the mind of the bobby-sox platoons, a "thing" combining, as one Southern Senator said, "The best qualities of Elvis Presley and Franklin D. Roosevelt." The jumpers were, in the beginning, teen-age girls who would bounce, jounce and jump as the cavalcade passed, squealing, "I seen him, I seen him." Gradually over the days their jumping seemed to grow more rhythmic, giving a jack-in-the-box effect of ups and downs in a thoroughly sexy oscillation. Then, as the press began to comment on the phenomenon, thus stimulating more artistic jumping, the middle-aged ladies began to jump up and down too, until, in the press bus following the candidate, one would note only the oddities: the lady, say, in her bathrobe, jumping back and forth; the heavily pregnant mother, jumping; the mother with a child in her arms, jumping; the row of nuns, all jiggling under their black robes, almost (but not quite) daring to jump; and the double-jumpers—teenagers who, as the cavalcade passed, would turn to face each other and, in ecstasy, place hands on each others' shoulders and jump up and down together as partnership. . . .

Jumping was only one form of response; so was noise; so was frenzy; so were sheer numbers. All reports of Kennedy response were authentic; what was wrong was that all predictions of a Kennedy sweep based on crowd response ignored an enormous political truth: that quiet people vote, too. . . .

. . . It was response that the press watched, and the response to Nixon and the response to Kennedy were entirely different. It was true indeed that Nixon commanded large crowds and several wild crowds—notably in Atlanta, in Philadelphia, in Texas. But the wildest of the Nixon demonstration always seemed to be indoor demonstrations where, one guessed, chiefly the Party faithful were assembled. In Cincinnati, Ohio; in Peoria, Illinois; in the New York Coliseum, the Republican leadership could mobilize its devoted ones, and they would shout and roar loud enough to match any band of Democrats. Yet out of doors the Nixon crowds were incomparably more subdued than the Kennedy crowds. Kennedy evoked an excitement, a response to personality. . . .

. . . Predominantly Democratic in orientation, the reporters who followed Nixon were, nonetheless, for the sake of their own careers, anxious to write as well, as vividly, as substantively as possible about him. Yet he held himself aloof; erratically he would sometimes permit reporters to ride his personal plane and at other times forbid it (Kennedy would as soon have dismissed his copilot as have dimissed the rotating trio of pool reporters who rode his personal plane everywhere); what he thought, what he planned, what he wished to express, Nixon kept to himself, believing (until too late in the campaign) that he could reach the American people over the heads of the press via television, or conscript press support from the publishers, who are proprietors of the press. (Mr. Nixon did, indeed, win the editorial support of 78 per cent of all newspapers whose publishers endorsed a candidate in 1960, along with the editorial support of all mass circulation magazines whose publishers chose sides.) What Mr. Nixon really felt, what he wished truly to clarify, he made no effort to communicate to the reporters, who were his amplifiers.

Nixon's personal distrust of the press colored the attitude of his press staff, too. His press secretary, Herbert Klein of San Diego, was an honest and kindly man—yet elusive, uninformative, colorless and withdrawn; he, too, appeared to be talking to the press with a sense of deep suspicion. Indeed, it was more difficult to elicit information from Klein than from John F. Kennedy himself. As much as any man, Klein was responsible for Nixon's bad press. To understand the inner Nixon, one had to reach Finch (the source of almost all the warm and positive information about the Vice-President) or Nixon's exceptionally able Planning Director, James Bassett (then assistant managing editor of the Los Angeles *Mirror*), who was, unfortunately, left behind in Washington throughout the campaign. At the beginning of the campaign the reporters assigned to Mr. Nixon were probably split down the middle between those friendly and those hostile to him; by the end of the campaign he had succeeded in making them predominantly into that which he had feared from the outset—hostile.

To be transferred from the Nixon campaign tour to the Kennedy campaign tour meant no lightening of exertion or weariness for any newspapermen—but it was as if one were transformed in role from leper and outcast to friend and battle companion.

The difference in attitudes to the press corps that one found on the Kennedy side reflected the attitude of its principal, too. For Kennedy, who enjoys words and reading, is a Pulitzer Prize winner himself and a one-time reporter; he has an enormous respect for those who work with words and those who write clean prose. He likes newspapermen and likes their company. Kennedy would, even in the course of the campaign, read the press dispatches, and if he particularly liked a passage, would tell the reporter or columnist that he had—and then quote from its phrases, in an amazing performance of memory and attention. Occasionally, early in the campaign, he would play a rather gay trick; one of his favorite stories was the story of a Colonel Davenport of Hartford, and Colonel Davenport's role in the writing of the Connecticut Constitution—he had told the story so many times that he knew he had drugged his following newsmen to inattention with its repetition. Therefore, now and then, he would substitute the name of one of the newspapermen for Colonel Davenport's name and refer, say, to a Colonel Bradlee, then cock his head to see if the correspondent mentioned had caught the change. He would ask advice of newspapermen—which, though he rarely followed it, flattered them nonetheless. Most of all he was available for quick exchanges of conversation—whether getting on his plane, or in his plane, or by the side of the road where he would stop to drink a Coca-Cola and then chat with the correspondents who clustered round. When presented, say, with a box of apples, he might fling one of them in an underarm pitch to a correspondent, to test whether the man was on his toes. He would borrow combs and pencils from the press—or accept chocolate bars (early in the primary campaigns) when his meal schedule also went awry.

The attitude of the candidate controlled his staff. His advisers rode the press buses and yielded a constant flow of information; his press staff of Pierre Salinger, Don Wilson and Andrew Hatcher gave off a sense of joy when they greeted a correspondent joining or rejoining the circuit, as if they had waited for him, and him alone, to arrive—and then whispered to him a little nugget of color or some anecdote that his particular magazine or newspaper would especially want. It was not only that they respected the press, but somehow as if they were part of the press—half hankering to be writing the dispatches and claiming the by-lines themselves.

There is no doubt that this kindliness, respect and cultivation of the press colored all the reporting that came from the Kennedy campaign, and the contrast colored adversely the reporting of the Nixon campaign. By the last weeks of the campaign, those forty or fifty national correspondents who had followed Kennedy since the beginning of his electoral exertions into the November days had become more than a press corps—they had become his friends and some of them, his most devoted admirers. When the bus or the plane rolled or flew through the night, they sang songs of their own composition about Mr. Nixon and the Republicans in chorus with the Kennedy staff and felt that they, too, were marching like soldiers of the Lord to the New Frontier. . . .

Chapter 9 ON THE INSIDE IN 1960

Attorney RICHARD N. GOODWIN (b. 1931)
wrote speeches for Kennedy in 1960 and held
several positions in the Kennedy Administration. In this excerpt from *Remembering America, A Voice From The Sixties* Goodwin
presents an insider's view of the presidential
race. How can one explain the devotion and
loyalty of those close to the candidate? Exactly why was Kennedy so successful on television?

"I don't mind sticking it to old Ike," said the senator as we sat on a bench in the
deserted Butler Aviation terminal at Washington's National Airport. It was a cold
January day in 1960, and Ted Sorensen and I had come to meet him on his return from
still another trip to the heartland, bringing with us a draft of the speech that was to be
the informal inauguration of Kennedy's presidential campaign. He had made the
formal announcement of his candidacy twelve days earlier, to a crowd of reporters,
family members, and staff gathered in the Senate Caucus Room. I was only in my third
month with the senator's staff, and this was my first participation in a major campaign
event.

Scheduled for delivery at the National Press Club, the speech was intended to

From *Remembering America, A Voice From The Sixties* by Richard N. Goodwin, copyright 1988 by
Blithedale Productions, Inc. Reprinted by permission of Little, Brown and Company and Sterling Lord
Literistic Inc.

describe Kennedy's view of the presidential office, a foundation for the message he would carry into the primary elections. Weeks of preparation, memos from presidential scholars, Kennedy's own statements and private reflections had been distilled into a dozen pages, which asserted, in a litany of forceful cliches, that the role of the president was to lead, morally and in action, to take initiatives and not just react to crisis, to revive a flagging America and draw the nation to new heights of grandeur. Wreathed with quotations from legendary heroes and scholars of repute, the address was not an exercise in political science. It was intended as contrast and rebuke to the Eisenhower presidency—then perceived as a time of listless drift, presided over by a man unwilling to intervene against a gradual deterioration of American strength and spirit. . . .

The polemic we might have written, the one that conveyed our true opinion, had been tailored to the political realities of the day. The speech did not mention Eisenhower by name. One could not attack "old Ike." Not personally. But the implications of Kennedy's address were clear. His call for new leadership to lift America from its corrosive complacency was an implicit but harsh accusation of Eisenhower failures.

Sorensen and I, our manuscript in hand, felt compelled to warn the weary candidate that the speech would be so interpreted. He did not even look up from the draft. Our admonitions were superfluous. The man could read. The man was smart. And his laconic rejoinder, the reflection of a course already set.

What choice did he have? A Democratic candidate had to run against the Republican record. His opponent would be Richard Nixon, whose greatest strength would be the popularity of his predecessor. Although Eisenhower was contemptuous of Nixon, whose own animosity toward the president who never wanted him was widely known, the two men were joined by the most powerful of political ties: self-interest. For Eisenhower, the election of a Republican successor would be a vindication of his leadership; and Nixon, like some infertile bride, had to rely on Eisenhower's teeming allurements to nurture his own fortunes into flower. (This was a reality that Nixon—in a now-familiar habit of self-delusion—would deny, until in the last desperate days of the campaign, he would at the price of some inward humiliation, ask Ike to campaign for him. Until then he had been determined to make it on his own, while the proud Eisenhower sat in the Oval Office waiting for the request that came only after it was too late. The enormous response to Eisenhower's last-minute emergence—ticker-tape parades, cheering crowds—made it clear that an earlier intervention would have put Nixon in the White House.)

For the next year, in hundreds of speeches, in continual assaults on the Republican party, on the Republican record, and on the Republican candidate, the name of Eisenhower was omitted. We even managed to find a way to accuse Nixon of having personally "lost Cuba" to Castro. On an earlier trip to that now-hostile island, the vice-president had praised the doomed Batista. That misguided support of a repressive dictatorship had fed the fires of anti-American revolution. Or so we said. Much later in the campaign, sitting in a hotel room during a trip to the barrens of Ohio, I handed Kennedy the draft of a detailed "documented" assault on the Republican loss of Cuba, the negligent establishment of a "communist base only ninety miles from our shores." Kennedy read the speech in silence, looked up, and remarked, musingly, "Of course, we don't say how we would have saved Cuba." Then, handing the speech back, unamended: "What the hell, they never told us how they would have saved China." . . . .

Sorensen and I were the only two speechwriters on the plane for the entire campaign, although others would make occasional contributions. Accompanying our travels was the bustling, talkative press secretary, Pierre Salinger, whose shrewdness and calculation were concealed by an almost clownlike, accommodating amiability intended to create an ambience of warmth and welcoming respect for the press corps, which conveyed our daily efforts to the nation. Dave Powers, friend and companion since John Kennedy's first campaign for Congress, called on a limitless store of anecdotes and street wisdom to provide the candidate with necessary diversion from the demands of the campaign, and his advice, never offered unless asked, was often decisive. Perhaps closest of all was the dour, taciturn Kenny O'Donnell—politician, personal confidant, Robert Kennedy's college roommate—who had no ambitions, no desires, no purpose that was not Kennedy's. One day, talking with Teddy White, Kennedy pointed to O'Donnell, stretched out sleeping across the seats: "You see Kenny, there. If I woke him up and asked him to jump out of this plane for me, he'd do it. You don't find that kind of loyalty easily."

Our entourage also included the political counselor Larry O'Brien; John Bailey, the Connecticut boss who had been among the first to support Kennedy's presidential hopes and would be rewarded with the chairmanship of the Democratic National Committee; and others whose names and roles have been amply recorded in the voluminous accounts of this most profusely recorded making of a president. If we were not exactly a "band of brothers," free from all jealousies, enmity, and the clash of ambitions, we had this in common: The candidate came first. Nothing could be done to disrupt his cause; no energy directed to a purpose but his. That was the one unforgivable sin.

We all knew it wouldn't be easy, but believed if we worked hard enough, refused all respite of body and mind, the reward was certain. We were convinced that our candidate was the best man, his summons a trumpet of truth, his cause infused with the moral imperatives of America. And on the other side was Nixon: treacherous opportunist, visionless, disliked even by the president he served. . . .

At the start of the campaign, sitting in the Senate office, Kennedy read a memo from economist John Kenneth Galbraith, describing the eight-year deterioration of economic growth and the present slide toward recession and unemployment. As he returned the last page to his desk, Kennedy looked up, grinning, and asked: "Do you know how I tell what is monetary and what is fiscal? Monetary begins with an M, and so does Martin of the Federal Reserve Board. How about that, Professor Galbraith?"

There would be plenty of experts eager to steer the candidate through the technical structures of economic policy, but it was the coal miners of West Virginia, not the professors of Harvard, who taught him that economic dissatisfaction derived from harsh realities. Four years of journeying to every part of the country had informed his intuition that confidence and pride in America had been undermined—by recession, by Khrushchev, by Castro, by an inchoate awareness of a vacancy in the soul of America. If the people loved Ike, it was partly because he was a personal emblem of a more glorious past, thus set apart from the incapacities of his administration.

Nixon's own campaign was—had to be—the mirror image of Kennedy's. He would run as the legitimate Republican heir to a popular Republican president. His large experience—senator, fierce adversary of communist conspiracy who had brought Alger Hiss to justice, vice-president for eight years, world traveler on comfortable terms with heads of foreign nations, tempered by personal debate with the volatile Khrushchev—was an imposing contrast to the greenhorn senator who had never held an executive office, whose own travels, with the exception of his service in the Pacific, were but the wanderings of a wealthy dilettante.

We disliked Nixon at the beginning, despised him by the end. "He's a filthy, lying son-of-a-bitch, and a very dangerous man," was among our candidate's kinder descriptions of his opponent in the closing weeks of the election. In part, Kennedy's remark was a natural reflection of a brutal political battle, but, obscenities aside, Kennedy had also come to sense that the man was truly dangerous, that his unique blend of intelligence and amorality might have devastating consequences for the country. . . .

By consensus—of staff, traveling press, and editorial commentary—Kennedy's confrontation with the suspicious ministers in Houston on that night of the Alliance for Progress's anonymous birth was a great success. "We have far more critical issues to face in the 1960 election," he began, "but because I am a Catholic and no Catholic has ever been elected president, the real issues in this campaign have been obscured . . . so it is apparently necessary for me to state once again—not what kind of church I believe in, for that should be important only to me—but what kind of America I believe in. I believe in an America where the separation of church and state is absolute . . . . where no religious body seeks to impose its will. . . . I want a Chief Executive whose public acts are responsible to all groups and obligated to none. . . . This is the kind of America I believe in and this is the kind my brother died for in Europe. And this is the kind of America for which our forefathers died when they fought for the Constitution and the Bill of Rights."

Kennedy had rarely been more impressive. His exposition, woven from appeals to constitutional principle and passionate assertions of personal belief, was more than enough to overturn any rational apprehension that his Catholic allegiance might menace Protestant and/or secular America. We were elated. We had met the enemy on his home grounds, and we had won. But, of course, it was not so simple. Neither reason nor honest passion could overcome fears rooted in childhood, absorbed from parents and neighbors who had themselves been shaped by the folk wisdom of earlier generations. In the country, as in West Virginia, people would overcome embedded prejudices only after they came to have confidence in the man, not his arguments.

Much later, in 1968, Eugene McCarthy told me that "if I'm elected, I'll be the first Catholic president"; meaning that Kennedy was only a nominal Catholic, born into a faith whose moral authority was ignored in the conduct of his daily life. "I remember on Fridays," Dave Powers told me, speaking of a time when Catholics were forbidden to eat meat on Friday, "Jack and I would wait till everyone was asleep and then sneak out for a hot dog." If true, it was a venial transgression, a trivial manifestation of a much larger truth: Jack Kennedy was among the most secular of men, his values derived not from his catechism, but from the mainstream of Western thought, Christian and pagan.

Yet he had been baptized at a Catholic font, faithfully observed the prescribed rituals of his Church, and thus had thrust upon him the burden of representing all of Catholic America—the legitimacy of their claim to a place of equal honor and dignity in the larger society. It was partly ironic. But no one was better suited to break the barrier. However, he would never completely overcome the issue of his religion. An upsurge of anti-Catholic sentiment in the closing days of the campaign turned most of the American heartland against his candidacy.

(Shortly after his election, riding down Fifth Avenue, Kennedy leaned out of the car window as he passed St. Patrick's Cathedral and waved toward the church. "Thanks," he said, "thanks a lot"). . . .

In every state the candidate would buy television time for a brief speech before a local assembly followed by a period of questions from the audience. But who was watching? And what did they hear? Not many, and not much. "Listen, Dave," Kennedy said to Dave Powers, "would you leave the bar in Charlestown [Massachusetts] to go watch a political speech? I sure as hell wouldn't." And the ratings confirmed his assertion. Even when we commandeered a national network, the average audience was less than ten million, most of them, we assumed, among the politically interested citizens who had already made up their minds.

"There's only one way we can break through the paper curtain," Kennedy had told us. "Television. At least people can listen to what I say, not what some reporter says I said. . . ." But we had already discovered that buying television time was not enough. We needed an audience. And, miraculously, Richard Nixon assured us an audience large enough to satisfy the most insatiable politician.

To Nixon, the decision to debate Kennedy must have seemed unavoidable, and perhaps it was. He had a lead, but a narrow one. A refusal to meet his adversary in personal combat might have been turned against him, used to cast doubt on his claims to superior knowledge, wisdom, and manly courage. Moreover, Nixon had, inevitably, been seduced by his own assaults on Kennedy's incapacities. ("Kennedy," Nixon told an intimate, "speaks over people's heads. I did pretty well with Khrushchev. I'll murder Kennedy.") He would beat him, and thus win the election on his own. Without Ike.

The debate was scheduled for September 26. The day before, the "issue team"—Ted Sorensen, Mike Feldman from our Washington office, and I—descended on Chicago to begin preparation. Since only two writers traveled with Kennedy continually, and I was by far the junior, it was my task to maneuver safely a large nylon suitcase and a footlocker—both crammed with memos, reprints, drafts, and reference material—from hotel room to plane and back again, each day of the campaign. To supplement our traveling files, Mike had prepared a ponderous volume fixed in a black binder, cataloging by issue virtually every recorded Nixon comment over the last several years. Fondly known to us as the "Nixopedia," the work was to supply material to attack the vice-president's frequent deceits and contradictions.

In the use of this reference material we were guided by a handful of instructions and comments scrawled on a note pad by Kennedy (still obedient to his throat doctor) during the preceding days: "We've got to recognize," he exhorted, "that he's just going to move from lie to lie about us in the next eight weeks. And we've got to get ours about him. I haven't said anything about him that's in error, except that he favored flexible price supports. Or, being 'a conservative at home—a revolutionary (liberal) abroad.' Then we say it can't be done. Wilson—Roosevelt—Truman succeeded abroad because they succeeded at home."

We worked through the night preparing index cards with single-sentence statements of Kennedy's position on a wide variety of domestic issues, some supporting facts, Nixon's probably position, and suggested rejoinders. As we labored, Kennedy was completing a campaign swing through nearby Ohio, where a perceptive listener might have guessed the candidate's mind was elsewhere. "It is possible for us to win Ohio and it is possible for us to lose Ohio," he told a partisan crowd at the Hotel Hollenback. (Kennedy, his brilliant political intuition still intact, was right as usual: We lost Ohio.)

The next morning, our unrested minds partially restored by several cups of coffee, we brought our heap of cards to Kennedy's suite, where the candidate, braced by a pair of pillows, sat in bed, alone, a discarded breakfast tray beside him, awaiting his assistants. With a voice-saving gesture he greeted us and reached for the products of our labor.

Throughout the morning he read the cards, stopping only to question the accuracy of our statements, substitute a more congenially phrased summation of his own, or ask for additional information. "Get Flemmings's statement on medical care," he instructed (Arthur Flemming was Eisenhower's secretary of health), "and show how ours would have cost less. We tied ours to a tax increase. He didn't." Every request sent one of us rushing from the room to search for files, or, if necessary, to telephone our "issue section" in Washington, captained by later Solicitor General Archibald Cox.

I was learning what it meant to be a professional. Tonight was it; the whole ball game. At least it might be. Yet there was no outward sign of tension, no reference to the import of the occasion, to disturb our subdued concentration on the particulars. We might as well have been preparing for a press conference in Albuquerque, except for the occasional appearance of family members who had, to this point, been pursuing their separate tasks. Bobby entered the suite, sat for about twenty minutes, left silently to check out the details of logistics and studio arrangements. Eunice, children in hand, came in, turned her cheek for a kiss, and then—"Come, children, Uncle Jack is busy"—left the room.

At lunchtime we returned to our rooms to revise the card, fill in gaps, rephrase statements—all in compliance with the candidate's laconic directions. As we left I saw Kennedy pick up the morning papers, looking—I presume—for late news reports that might be mentioned during the evening's discussion. On our return, we again reviewed the range of possible questions, Kennedy silently absorbing our work and explanatory comments, rehearsing only in the privacy of his own mind.

Ted Sorensen handed him the draft of suggested opening statement. "Too rhetorical," he said, "let me give it a try," motioning us to leave the room while he dictated to Evelyn Lincoln, his personal secretary; recalling us about forty minutes later to take the newly typed draft with instructions "clean it up"; and then, the debate only a few hours away, announcing, "I'm going to take a nap; be back here around seven." On returning to my room, I found that I had left some of my notes in the candidate's suite. I returned, entering on tiptoe—candidates did not then have Secret Service guards to obstruct intruders; that protection was provided only after Robert Kennedy's assassination—and walked to the oval glass table where the debris of the day's work was strewn. The suite was silent. He's actually sleeping, I thought wonderingly, then glimpsed Eunice and her children entering behind me. A whispered maternal comment triggered a sudden, loud exchange between the children. There was a roar from the inner bedroom—"What the hell's going on out there?" I ran, never looking back. The sister could take care of herself.

Meanwhile, on another Chicago street, Richard Nixon spent the day in his hotel room, alone with his thoughts. He too was a professional, unwilling to reveal outward signs of strain, but choosing to protect himself from observation not through inner discipline, but by seclusion behind closed doors. In the studio that night, Nixon would pace along the slightly raised stage in short, nervous steps, occasionally arousing himself to a forced, barely comprehensible, attempt at humor.

The debate less than a hour away, we reentered the candidate's suite. Bobby was already there, along with Kenny O'Donnell and Dave Powers. We handed him a freshly typed, "cleaned up" copy of his opening statement. "How about makeup?" Bobby asked. "There's a man here." "I don't think so," Kennedy replied, "just some talcum," and entered the bathroom to brush some Mennen over his naturally—or pharmaceutically—sanguine features.

I sat with a small group of staff members before a television set, elation mounting as the debate unfolded. Our man was, as we had anticipated, in command of his material, calm, his serious intensity of conviction occasionally interrupted by flashes of humor. He could have been talking to a small group in a friendly living room. And he was. To millions of groups; in millions of rooms.

But Nixon!

Admittedly he knew his answers, was quick to prod Kennedy's presumed vulnerabilities. But the camera showed something else: a man strangely severed from his own shrewd, reasoned discourse. Facial muscles tensed, sweat appearing on brow and cheeks, lips occasionally forced into a smile unrelated to his words, Nixon appeared more like a losing football coach summoned before the board of trustees than a leader of the free world. Afterward analysts and apologists would blame Nixon's dismaying appearance on his makeup, the lighting, the erroneous advice of technicians. But we knew better. The country sensed it. What we saw on Nixon's face that night was the panic in his soul.

As the moderator signed off, our small band erupted in cheers. I was jubilant. It was over! We had won! Not just the debate. We had won the election!

Leaving the studio, Kennedy departed for the airport where an ebullient campaign staff greeted him with applause as he boarded the *Caroline* for a flight to Hellriegel's Inn in Painesville, Ohio, where he was to give a breakfast speech pledging full employment for the workers of that industrial state. Relaxing with a beer and a bowl of tomato soup, Kennedy, although physically and mentally exhausted, was clearly satisfied with his night's work. Almost compulsively, as if unwilling to admit the debate was over, he rehearsed his answers and those of Nixon with almost total recall. "We'll need something better on education," he said, as if already preparing for the next debate, or just as likely, inwardly trying to reedit the hour that had just passed. To me it all seemed too subdued, too matter-of-fact. We had beaten the bastard, hadn't we; nothing could stop us now. Yet we all restrained our shared elation in deference to Kennedy's own behavior. Finally, unable to hold back, I blurted, "We've got it won now." Kennedy looked up, smiled. "It was all right," he said and returned to his soup.

It was far from over. Whatever lead the debate had produced would gradually diminish toward virtual extinction by election eve. But the campaign had entered a new dimension. The attacks on Kennedy's youth, immaturity, and inexperience had been answered and destroyed as the cameras revealed, in Teddy White's words, a man who, "obviously, in flesh and blood . . . . was the Vice-President's equal." And not just equal; more authentic, more American as Americans would like themselves to be.

The campaign had been stripped of deceptive irrelevancies, except for the indestructible issue of religion. Nixon had forfeited his most telling issues. From now on it would be Democrat against Republican, Kennedy's summons to hazardous greatness against Nixon's assurance of progressive continuity, man against man. You paid your money and took your choice, or rather, you cast your vote and took your chance.

And though we had not yet shredded the "paper curtain," the debate had made a substantial tear. The crowds that lined the streets and filled the halls swelled in numbers, responding to the candidate with mounting, often near-hysterical intensity. In a single night, television had created its first political celebrity.

Part Three THE COMMUNICATOR

Chapter 10 THE INAUGURAL ADDRESS

President Kennedy's Inaugural Address has been highly acclaimed for its inspiring rhetoric. What specifically does it promise? What exactly does it seek from the American people? Does it challenge postwar assumptions about U.S.-Soviet relations?

We observe today not a victory of party but a celebration of freedom—symbolizing an end as well as a beginning—signifying renewal as well as change. For I have sworn before you and Almighty God the same solemn oath our forebears prescribed nearly a century and three-quarters ago.

The world is very different now. For man holds in his mortal hands the power to abolish all forms of human poverty and all forms of human life. And yet the same revolutionary belief for which our forebears fought is still at issue around the globe, the belief that the rights of man come not from the generosity of the state but from the hand of God.

We dare not forget today that we are the heirs of that first revolution. Let the word go forth from this time and place, to friend and place, to friend and foe alike, that the torch has been passed to a new generation of Americans—born in this century,

From *Public Papers Of The Presidents Of the United States, John F. Kennedy...January 20 to December 31, 1961* tempered by war, disciplined by a hard and bitter peace, proud of our ancient heritage—and unwilling to witness or permit the slow undoing of those human rights to which this nation has always been committed, and to which we are committed today at home and around the world.

Let every nation know, whether it wishes us well or ill, that we shall pay any price, bear any burden, meet any hardship, support any friend, oppose any foe to assure the survival and the success of liberty.

This much we pledge—and more.

To those old allies whose cultural and spiritual origins we share, we pledge the loyalty of faithful friends. United, there is little we cannot do in a host of cooperative ventures. Divided, there is little we can do—for we dare not meet a powerful challenge at odds and split asunder.

To those new states whom we welcome to the ranks of the free, we pledge our word that one form of colonial control shall not have passed away merely to be replaced by a far more iron tyranny. We shall not always expect to find them supporting our view. But we shall always hope to find them strongly supporting their own freedom—and to remember that, in the past, those who foolishly sought power by riding the back of the tiger ended up inside.

To those peoples in the huts and villages of half the globe struggling to break the bonds of mass misery, we pledge our best efforts to help them help themselves, for whatever period is required, not because the Communists may be doing it, not because we seek their votes, but because it is right. If a free society cannot help the many who are poor, it cannot save the few who are rich.

To our sister republics south of our border, we offer a special pledge—to convert our good words into good deeds—in a new alliance for progress, to assist free men and free governments in casting off the chains of poverty. But this peaceful revolution of hope cannot become the prey of hostile powers. Let all our neighbors know that we shall join with them to oppose aggression or subversion anywhere in the Americas. And let every other power know that this hemisphere intends to remain the master of its own house.

To that world assembly of sovereign states, the United Nations, our last best hope in an age where the instruments of war have far outpaced the instruments of peace, we renew our pledge of support—to prevent it from becoming merely a forum for invective—to strengthen its shield of the new and the weak—and to enlarge the area in which its writ may run.

Finally, to those nations who would make themselves our adversary, we offer not a pledge but a request: that both sides begin anew the quest for peace, before the dark powers of destruction unleashed by science engulf all humanity in planned or accidental self-destruction.

We dare not tempt them with weakness. For only when our arms are sufficient beyond doubt can we be certain beyond doubt that they will never be employed.

But neither can two great and powerful groups of nations take comfort from our present course—both sides overburdened by the cost of modern weapons, both rightly alarmed by the steady spread of the deadly atom, yet both racing to alter that uncertain balance of terror that stays the hand of mankind's final war.

So let us begin anew—remembering on both sides that civility is not a sign of weakness, and sincerity is always subject to proof. Let us never negotiate out of fear, but let us never fear to negotiate.

Let both sides explore what problems unite us instead of belaboring those problems which divide us.

Let both sides, for the first time, formulate serious and precise proposals for the inspection and control of arms—and bring the absolute power to destroy other nations under the absolute control of all nations.

Let both sides seek to invoke the wonders of science instead of its terrors. Together let us explore the stars, conquer the deserts, eradicate disease, tap the ocean depths and encourage the arts and commerce.

Let both sides unite to heed in all corners of the earth the command of Isaiah—to "undo the heavy burdens . . . . [and] let the oppressed go free."

And if a beach-head of cooperation may push back the jungle of suspicion, let both sides join in creating a new endeavor, not a new balance of power, but a new world of law, where the strong are just and weak secure and the peace preserved.

All this will not be finished in the first one hundred days. Nor will it be finished in the first one thousand days, nor in the life of this Administration, nor even perhaps in our lifetime on this planet. But let us begin.

In your hands, my fellow citizens, more than mine, will rest the final success or failure of our course, Since this country was founded, each generation of Americans has been summoned to give testimony to its national loyalty. The graves of young Americans who answered the call to service surround the globe.

Now the trumpet summons us again—not as a call to bear arms, though arms we need—not as a call to battle, though embattled we are—but a call to bear the burden of a long twilight struggle, year in and year out, "rejoicing in hope, patient in tribulation"—a struggle against the common enemies of man: tyranny, poverty, disease and war itself.

Can we forge against these enemies a grand and global alliance, North and South, East and West, that can assure a more fruitful life for all mankind? Will you join in that historic effort?

In the long history of the world, only a few generations have been granted the role of defending freedom in its hour of maximum danger. I do not shrink from this responsibility—I welcome it. I do not believe that any of us would exchange places with any other people or any other generation. The energy, the faith, the devotion which we bring to this endeavor will light our country and all who serve it—and the glow from that fire can truly light the world.

And so, my fellow Americans, ask not what your country can do for you—ask what you can do for your country.

My fellow citizens of the world, ask not what America will do for you, but what together we can do for the freedom of man.

Finally, whether you are citizens of America or citizens of the world, ask of us here the same high standards of strength and sacrifice which we ask of you. With a good conscience our only sure reward, with history the final judge of our deeds, let us go forth to lead the land we love, asking His blessing and His help, but knowing that here on earth God's work must truly be our own.

Chapter 11 THE PRESIDENT AND THE MASS MEDIA

PIERRE SALINGER (b. 1925) was President Kennedy's press secretary. Since 1983 he has been chief foreign correspondent for ABC News. In this selection from *With Kennedy*, he tells us more about the President's unprecedented skill with the media. Why does Kennedy appear to be so willing to be accessible to reporters?

The combination of wire services and networks enabled the President to communicate with unbelievable speed both to the nation and the world. Ten minutes after I gave a presidential statement of major significance, it would be on the air and on the teletype machines of newspapers here and abroad. There were desperate moments during the Cuban missile crisis when communications between JFK and Khrushchev were running hours behind because of the total inadequacy of diplomatic channels. We decided to release JFK's statements directly to the networks and wire services, knowing that Moscow was monitoring our radio frequencies and news wires and would have the word hours faster. Krushchev did the same with Radio Moscow and Tass, and the speed-up in communications may very well have been a factor in preventing escalation of the crisis. This necessity for instantaneous communication

From *With Kennedy* by Pierre Salinger, copyright 1966 by Pierre Salinger. Used by permission of Doubleday, a division of Bantam, Doubleday, Dell Publishing Group, Inc., and Sterling Lord Agency.

was the reason for prompt agreement, after the Cuban crisis, on installation of the hot line (teletype system) between Washington and Moscow.

JFK gave television some other very important advantages in addition to the televised press conference.

On at least two occasions, television cameras were permitted to follow him around in his daily work, giving the American people an unprecedented view of the President at work. One of these occasions resulted in the ABC television program *Crisis*, which showed the President and Attorney General Robert F. Kennedy actually in discussion in their offices making the important decisions on what to do to integrate the University of Alabama. The fact that Alabama's Governor George C. Wallace also allowed the cameras for the same show access to his decision making meetings resulted in as important a view of the American presidency in action as television has ever been able to present.

The President also granted exclusive interviews to television. The sole criterion for such an interview was that the request contain an idea of some merit. An outstanding example was the President's interview with David Schoenbrun of CBS, a difficult but erudite reporter. Schoenbrun was the greatest expert in the press on the subject of the European Common Market. The President had started the year 1962 by sending to the Congress an extremely complicated piece of legislation to facilitate United States trade relations with its allies—particularly the Common Market. At the time the bill was sent to Congress, a very small percentage of the American people even knew of the existence of the Market, and fewer still of its importance to American export and import trade. The President used this interview with Schoenbrun to give a clear and incisive analysis of the United States trade pattern and to explain the importance of doing business with the Common Market. This was just one phase of a vast educational campaign conducted by the government on this important point.

Walter Cronkite of CBS also had an exclusive interview with JFK to kick off the network's change-over from a fifteen- to a thirty-minute evening news show. But this one had an unfortunate aftermath. CBS shot half an hour of questions and answers, mostly on Vietnam, but cut the footage to twelve minutes for actual broadcast. The result was a partial distortion of JFK's opinion of President Ngo Dinh Diem.

In the actual interview, which was filmed, President Kennedy spoke of his respect and sympathy for the problems of President Diem. When the film was shown to the public, only the unfavorable presidential remarks remained, and JFK's praise of Diem had been deleted.

The impression was left that JFK had no confidence at all in Diem, and when he and his brother, Ngo Dinh Nhu, were later shot to death in a military coup, there were persistent charges from Madame Nhu and others that the President's statements had given aid and comfort to Diem's enemies. JFK was deeply hurt by the accusations.

The president also gave an exclusive to NBC's Huntley-Brinkley show when it went to thirty minutes. It also had to be cut to fit their time format, but this time JFK was insistent that the White House have final approval of what was shown on the air, and NBC agreed.

The most dramatic of JFK's appearances, *A Conversation With the President*, was seen and heard on all TV and radio networks on the evening of December 17, 1962. His own office was the setting for the informal, hour-long conversation with Lawrence of ABC, Herman of CBS, and Vanocur of NBC. An audience of tens of millions heard his candid appraisal of the triumphs and disappointments of his first two years in office. Never before had the American public had such an intimate glimpse of a President: his personality, his mind at work, his sense of history—and his sense of humor.

The most penetrating answer on the President's attitudes and feelings about his job was elicited by a question from Bill Lawrence in which he asked:

"As you look back upon your first two years in office, sir, has your experience in the office matched your expectations? You had studied a good deal the power of the presidency, the methods of its operations. How has this worked out as you saw it in advance?"

The President's answer was very revealing. "Well, I think in the first place the problems are more difficult than I had imagined they were. Secondly there is a limitation upon the ability of the United States to solve these problems. We are involved now in the Congo in a very difficult situation. We have been unable to secure an implementation of the policy which we have supported. We are involved in a good many other areas. We are trying to see if a solution can be found to the struggle between Pakistan and India, with whom we want to maintain friendly relations. Yet they are unable to come to an agreement. There is a limitation, in other words, upon the power of the United States to bring about solutions.

"I think our people get awfully impatient and maybe fatigued and tired, and saying 'We have been carrying this burden for seventeen years; can we lay it down?' We can't lay it down, and I don't see how we are going to lay it down in this century.

"So that I would say that the problems are more difficult than I had imagined them to be. The responsibilities placed on the United States are greater than I imagined them to be, and there are greater limitations upon our ability to bring about a favorable result than I had imagined them to be. And I think that is probably true of anyone who becomes President, because there is such a difference between those who advise or speak or legislate, and between the man who must select from the various alternatives proposed and say that this shall be the policy of the United States. It is much easier to make the speeches than it is to finally make the judgments, because unfortunately your advisers are frequently divided. If you take the wrong course, and on occasion I have, the President bears the burden of the responsibility quite rightly. The advisers may move on to new advice. . . ."

Because of the huge readership of magazines such as *Life, Look, McCall's, The Saturday Evening Post, Ladies' Home Journal, Good Housekeeping, Redbook,* and others, their writers had special access to the Kennedys. The most memorable magazine spread of the Kennedy years was *Look's* "The President and His Son," the marvelous pictures of JFK playing with John in his office. When writer Laura Bergquist and photographer Stanley Tretick first came to me with the idea, Mrs. Kennedy was dead set against it. She felt it was too much an invasion of the family's privacy. The President smiled when I told him of her objections.

"Let's hold off on it for a while, then," he said. "We'll take another look at it the next time she leaves town."

A week or two later, Mrs. Kennedy went to Italy and Miss Bergquist and Tretick spent two hours in the President's office shooting the pictures that were to break a nation's heart when they ran in *Look* the very week of the assassination.

When Mrs. Kennedy came back from Italy and I told her what we had done, she was very upset with me.

"Wait and see, you'll love the pictures," I told her.

"You always say that," was her crisp reply. . . .

Superimposed on the White House establishment was another very important segment of the Washington press—the influential columnists whose words are read daily throughout the United States.

The ranking members of his fraternity were James (Scotty) Reston of the New York *Times*, Walter Lippmann, Joseph and Stewart Alsop, Marquis Childs, Doris Fleeson, William S. White, Rowland Evans and Robert Novak, Joseph Kraft and Drew Pearson.

Because of their influence throughout the country, most of these columnists got special treatment. A request from one of them to see the President personally was usually honored, and White House staff members at the policy level like Ted Sorensen and McGeorge Bundy made sure that they had the administration's views on prevailing problems.

In any crisis situation, it was standard operating procedure to be in touch with these columnists to give them background on the government's actions. The President, himself, frequently took part in these background sessions. He would, for example, call Lippman or invite him to the White House.

I made it a point to lunch with these correspondents from time to time to find out what their problems were and to keep them abreast of the administration's thinking. . . .

I also felt very strongly that the President himself should be more accessible to the press. He was, without question, the most articulate and persuasive Chief Executive since FDR. He had bold and controversial concepts for moving the nation ahead that had to be sold both to the Congress and to the public, and no one could sell them more effectively than he. I found him totally receptive to my suggestion that he remove many of the traditional obstacles that have stood between the President and the press. The rule against live television at his press conferences was but the first barrier to go. His greater availability for exclusive interviews on TV and in all other media was another advance. He was also to surpass all other Presidents in the number of briefings, or backgrounders, he held in his office with large numbers of reporters—

both foreign and American. Many of his comments were off-the-record, but they gave the press a clear reading of his attitudes and objectives. Because of such briefings, he was able to reduce substantially the publication or broadcast of false or misleading speculation that could react to his disadvantage both at home and abroad.

The President came up with the idea of inviting the country's leading publishers to lunch on a state-by-state basis. My office made up the lists of invitees for the twenty-five such lunches he held. Usually we would take the twenty or so largest papers in the state. (With the small size of the states these got down to papers with a circulation of barely 10,000 people.) Then to fill out the lunch, we would invite the officers of that particular state's weekly press association. This gave the President a good cross section of the state's press.

The lunch would be preceded by a short cocktail session. The President would come in as lunchtime approached and go around and shake hands with each of the publishers personally. At the lunches in the State Dining Room, the President would converse with his neighbors at the table until dessert was served. Then he would give a short review of his views on current domestic and international affairs. At the close of his talks, he would open up the luncheon for discussion.

These discussions were wide in nature, but there was virtually no discussion on the role of the press and the White House. During 1961, the principal subjects were Cuba and Berlin. In 1962, the subjects of the greatest interest were taxes and foreign trade. . . .

The publishers were generally pleased with the President's frankness and with the honor of being invited to the White House for lunch. My files are full of letters from publishers who, on arriving home, wrote to say they had a far better understanding of the President and his problems than they had had before. One wrote me: "I will never be able to write another glib editorial attacking the President without thinking of that lunch and the great burdens of an American President . . . ."

Looking back on it now, the decision to open the press conference to live TV was a proper one. President Johnson, to be certain, doesn't use the format as often as President Kennedy did, but for reasons that have nothing to do with its effectiveness. He simply feels more comfortable—and more communicative—in a less hectic atmosphere. . . .

There can be no question that it was right for JFK. The ideas and philosophy of the man were best displayed during those moments of truth when he stood alone before millions of his countrymen to answer the questions of greatest moment to their lives and their very survival. Lacking the memoirs JFK would surely have written, the transcripts of his press conference become his most revelatory legacy. They reveal as much about the man as they do about his ideas. His grasp of the infinite detail of government; his studied refusal to look at problems in over-simple terms; his quickness of mind; his capacity for righteous anger; and his quick humor are all clearly evident. . . .

One particular televised press conference of the President opened up another—and highly exciting—vista. It was the only press conference of the President carried live to Europe by the communication satellite, Telstar.

If anyone has any doubts that the installation of a full communications satellite system is going to revolutionize the world from an information standpoint, they have only to see what happened on this particular occasion.

During the first months of the administration, the President had been asked a number of times whether he was going to devalue the American dollar or raise the price of gold. He had emphatically denied both of these rumors, with absolutely no effect on foreign gold markets.

On the occasion of this particular press conference, the President was again asked the same question. He gave them the same answer; no devaluation, no rise in the gold price. The results on the London gold market were staggering. They caused an immediate break in London gold prices as investors and speculators saw the President in person, live on television, making the statement.

Thousands of words written in newspapers had not had this effect, but the sight of the President making the statement did.

President Kennedy was amazed by the reaction his words had in England. But it also proved to him that a President of the United States could bring about massive support for his policies, if only he could be seen and heard directly. It made him a full supporter of the communications satellite concept—which is now rapidly progressing toward reality. . . .

Chapter 12 THE MANIPULATOR

BENJAMIN C. BRADLEE (b. 1921) was a close friend of the President's during the Thousand Days and was also a senior editor and Washington bureau chief of *Newsweek*. Since 1965 he has been with the *Washington Post*. Here Bradlee recalls a Kennedy who is quite unlike the near-saint portrayed by Schlesinger, Sorensen, Salinger and other loyalists. How did Kennedy manipulate Bradlee? What does the President's use of classified documents reveal about him?

By 1960 I had been a cub reporter, a police reporter, a court reporter, a foreign correspondent, and a political reporter for fourteen years. I had spent a majority of these years outside of Washington, in New Hampshire and in Paris. As a result, I had fewer politicians as friends than most of my colleagues and all of my competitors, and I worried about it. This thing I had going with the junior senator from Massachusetts was very seductive. He had the smell of success, and my special access to him was enormously valuable to *Newsweek*, in whose Washington bureau I was then working. And I truly liked him; our wives were becoming friends; we ate and drank together.

I never wrote less than I knew about him, filing the good with the bad. But obviously, the information Kennedy gave me tended to put him and his policies in a favorable light, even though all such information was passed through special filters, in the first instance by me, and to a greater extent by *Newsweek*'s editors. If I was had, so be it; I doubt I will ever be so close to a political figure again. If I should get that close again, there will be nothing missing from my record of conversations.

The minor gap in the record began in August, 1962, when *Look* magazine published an article by Fletcer Knebel entitled "Kennedy vs. The Press," and subtitled "Never have so few bawled out so many so often for so little, as the Kennedys battle reporters." In the light of the Nixon experience, and in light of the simple, historic fact that John Kennedy enjoyed better relations with the press than any other president since Mergenthaler invented the linotype, the hyperbole here is hard to believe. But the immediate problem for me centered on two paragraphs in the story, plus some bit of graphic hyperbole by *Look*'s art director, entitled "They've Dueled with Kennedy" beneath an old woodcut of a bearded man in a three-quarter length coat, left hand behind his back, right hand with pistol raised at the ready.

The paragraphs at issue read as follows:

Even a good friend of the President, Benjamin C. Bradlee, Washington bureau chief of *Newsweek*, felt the presidential fire. Kennedy phoned him to take him to task for a *Newsweek* story about an old Massachusetts aide of Kennedy's being considered for a federal judgeship. Also ticked off later by Attorney General Kennedy for another story, Bradlee takes the rebukes philosophically and not too seriously.

'It's almost impossible,' he says, 'to write a story they like. Even if a story is quite favorable to their side, they'll find on paragraph to quibble with.'

Would anyone believe I thought that quote was off the record? Anyway, I said it, and of course it was true. Kennedys by definition want 110 percent from their friends, especially their friends in the press, and feel cheated by anything less. I do remember Kennedy called to complain about the "old Massachusetts aide." That was Francis Xavior Morrissey, a municipal (pronounced MU-ni-SIP-ple in Boston) court judge, whose legal abilities were taxed by parking ticket cases, and whom Kennedy was trying to slip unnoticed onto the federal bench. And I remember what the president of the United States said, "Jesus Christ, you guys are something else. When I was elected you all said that my old man would run the country in consultation with the pope. Now here's the only thing he's ever asked me to do for him, and you guys piss all over me."

I have no recollection of the particular incident that ticked off the attorney general.

The graphics included two boxes containing lists of names of journalists, one called "Jumped on by Jack," and the other "Bawled out by Bobby." My name was the only one to make both lists.

This really irritated the president of the United States. Later he was to explain: "Jesus, there you are really plugged in, better than any other reporter except Charlie (Bartlett), getting one exclusive after another out of this place, and what do you do but dump all over us." To make matters worse, John Denson, editor of the *New York*

Herald Tribune, latched on to the story and ordered the *Tribune*'s Washington bureau chief, Robert Donovan, to interview all of us historians in the doghouse. Hugh Sidey of *Time* had the good sense to bail out of trouble by saying that the Kennedys may gripe a little but they are the best news sources in history. When Donovan called me, I felt I was already in hopelessly hot water with the Kennedys and was quoted only as saying that I declined to comment.

And that did it. From regular contact—dinner at the White House once and sometimes twice a week, and telephone calls as needed in either direction—to no contact. The next time we saw the Kennedys was in November, three months later, when Jackie invited my wife, Tony, and the children over for movies and lollipops. A few days later Kennedy and Tony were talking at a dance about how hard it was to be friends with someone who wrote everything he knew, and we were pals again.

It seems strange now, so many years later, that a friendship like ours could not survive such a minor irritant. Some of the reasons have their roots in that wonderful law of the Boston Irish political jungle: "Don't get mad; get even." He never got mad, but he plainly got even, cutting me out of a mainstream of information that had been enormously valuable to me and to *Newsweek*. At issue, then and later, was the question that plagued us both: What, in fact, was I? A friend, or a journalist? I wanted to be both. And whereas I think Kennedy valued my friendship—I made him laugh, I brought him the fruits of contact with an outside world from which he was now shut out—he valued my journalism most when it carried his water. . . .

September 14, 1962/ I saw the president in Newport briefly this morning, for the first time since I had been banished for my part in the *Look* magazine critique of the Kennedys and the press. We exchanged an absolute minimum of words over an elapsed time of perhaps twenty minutes. I was greeted with "Oh, hi. How've you been?" In the middle of "conversation," he said "That's fine" a couple of times. And at the end, he asked after Tony and said, "See you later."

I had been nervous about seeing him again—after three months in the doghouse. In a strange way, I understood why he was sore . . . . it was hard to make new friends once those White House doors had closed behind you, and if old friends wanted to be friends *and* reporters, maybe the two couldn't mix. I wanted to be friends again. I missed the access, of course, but I missed the laughter and the warmth just as much. What I couldn't and wouldn't do was send a message over the stone wall, saying I had learned my lesson. Anyway the freeze is obviously still on.

The occasion for this brief encounter was the sequel, at last, of the case of "John's Other Wife." Most Washington correspondents, or at least most of those with any involvement in covering the White House had been familiar with the broad outlines of the case for months. And yet no responsible newspaper or magazine had written one word about it.

Some anti-Semitic, racist hate sheets had published stories, however, ("Kennedy's Divorce Exposed! Is Present Marriage Valid? Excommunication Possible") and I felt *Newsweek* could be first with the story if we backed into it by writing about the hate sheets themselves in the Press section, how they were spreading the story, and who was financing them. I approached Salinger with the idea, but told him I would need some solid FBI documentation about the character of the organizations and people involved in spreading the Blauvelt story.

A couple of days later, Salinger called me with the following proposition: If I agreed to show the president the finished story, and if I got my tail up to Newport where he was vacationing, he would deliver a package of the relevant FBI documents to a Newport motel and let me have them for a period not to exceed twenty-four hours. It was specifically understood that I was not to xerox anything in the FBI files, that I was not to indicate in any way that I had been given access to FBI files (I never had been given such access before, and I have never been given such access since), and that in case of a lawsuit, I would not be given access to these files a second time. I checked with *Newsweek*'s editor, Oz Elliott, and we decided to go ahead, despite a reluctance to give anyone, even the president of the United States, the right of approval of anything we wrote. In effect, we were giving Kennedy what he later said he liked so much "the right of clearance." This is a right all presidents covet, but which they should normally not be given. This one time, the book seemed worth the candle, however, and we decided to strike the deal.

Chuck Roberts, *Newsweek*'s White House correspondent, and I got on the next plane to Newport via Providence, and went right to the motel. The FBI files arrived soon afterwards, late in the afternoon, and we stayed up all night long, first reading everything in the files, then writing the story.

"Ever since the heyday of yellow journalism" the story in the magazine's Press section began, "the sense of responsibility of the American press has been more censured than praised. For political profit or for readers' pennies, sensation has often triumphed over reliability."

"But for the last 16 months, virtually every major newspaper, magazine and wire service in the U.S. has refused to publish a sensational report—familiar to hundreds of thousands of Americans—about the president of the United States. They have spiked the story despite what appears to be 'documentary evidence' and despite scattered publication of it, or hints at it, by hate groups and gossip columnists."

"The 'story' falsely alleges that before he married Jacqueline Bouvier in Newport, R.I. on Sept. 12, 1953, John F. Kennedy was secretly married to a two-time divorcee."

The story went on to describe the organizations that were spreading the story . . . an Alabama hate sheet called "The Thunderbolt"; an Arkansas racist sheet called "The Winrod Letter," which had distributed hundreds of thousands of specially photostated four-page folders entitled "The Blauvelt Family Genealogy"; the Christian Education Association, headed by Condé McGinley, publisher of what the FBI called "the vitriolic hate sheet 'Common Sense' "; the "Right Brigade," described by Cleveland police as a "crackpot" organization; and a Holyoke, Mass., paper company whose mailings were handled by an associate of Robert Welch, founder of the John Birch Society.

At eight o'clock the next morning, as planned, I took the finished piece over to Hammersmith Farm, the Auchincloss summer mansion, where the Kennedys were vacationing to watch the America's Cup races, returned the FBI files to Salinger, and got the president's ok. As I was leaving his office with Kennedy, we bumped into the Ormsby-Gores, who were joining the Kennedys to watch the yacht races. The British ambassador smiled politely and asked if I were joining them for the races.

"No," Kennedy answered quickly. "He's not coming." And he meant it. . . .

April 10, 1963/ "Here it is," the president said, shoving a fat file at me across his desk this afternoon, "Eyes Only, Secret and Everything." I was there to get the story behind Canadian Prime Minister Diefenbaker's charges that the president of the United States had written "S.O.B." on some official State Department document concerning Diefenbaker and Canada.

The key document, classified Secret, is a memorandum from Walt Rostow to the president outlining what the State Department hoped to accomplish during Kennedy's visit to Canada in May, 1961. U.S. policy, Rostow argued, should be to "push" the Canadians: 1) to increase their Alliance for Progress contribution; 2) to join the Organization of American States; 3) to increase their foreign aid contribution and involvement, especially with the Indian consortium; and 4) to do more with the Neutrality Commission policing the uneasy truce in Laos.

One year later, in May 1962, in a long, extraordinary letter to George Ball, who was then acting secretary of state, the U.S. ambassador to Canada, Livingston Merchant, described a ranting conversation he had had with Diefenbaker in which the Canadian p.m. revealed that he now possessed the original Rostow document (Kennedy guesses that someone on the U.S. delegation must have left it at a session with the Canadians, probably Bundy), that the letters "S.O.B." in the president's handwriting were on the document; that he and all Canadians would resent that, plus the word "push" if the document were made public; and that he intended to make it public as part of his political campaign for reelection. He told Merchant he had to release the document because Pearson and the Liberals were campaigning as the favorite party of the Kennedy administration, and Pearson himself had been to the White House for the Nobel Prize winner's dinner, and had seen Kennedy privately for half an hour beforehand. Diefenbaker was practically out of his mind with rage, Merchant reported.

The State Department's instructions back to Merchant four days later, closely following a special memorandum by Bundy and Ball, ordered the U.S. ambassador to go back to Diefenbaker and tell him that he would relay no such message to his government, especially to Kennedy, out of respect for Canada and Diefenbaker. Merchant was told to describe in detail what the U.S. reaction would be to this blackmail, and to tell Diefenbaker that Kennedy would not see him under any conditions, as Merchant had suggested.

Merchant reported back that it was his opinion that Diefenbaker, though still furious, would not release the document. And there the story lies. The president told me he did not write "S.O.B." "At that time," Kennedy added, "I didn't think Diefenbaker was a son of a bitch. (Pause, for effect.) I thought he was a prick."

Kennedy wondered why the Canadian prime minister "didn't do what any normal, friendly government would do . . . make a photostatic copy, and return the original."

Act II of the steel crisis was also on Kennedy's mind, especially the coincidence of the dates, exactly one year after Act I, when U.S. Steel raised its prices, followed the next day by five other major steel manufacturers raising theirs. The president feels that his office and authority are being flouted, but he seems unsure what he should do about it, or can do about it. Basically, he feels the steel people are impossible. He called them "those fuckers." A labor-management committee to work out a formula whereby some porton of a price increase would go to labor as its share, Kennedy said, might be possible if you were dealing with normal people, but not with steel people. The *Newsweek* expert on prices had doubted that the market would support a price rise at this time, but Kennedy dismissed that argument. "If foreign steel is imported," he said, "that would mean a loss of jobs here, and steel would then be hitting me over the head with other weapons." Kennedy revealed there was a special White House meeting at 6:00 that night, and called a man named "John" to ask him to be present.

On Laos, he again said there wasn't much the U.S. could do. He said we were moving up some supplies to Kong Le, but noted the irony of now putting all the American eggs in the basket of Souvanna Phouma, the man the Eisenhower administration had tried to descredit as a Communist.

The president was most interested in *Newsweek*'s story, by Paris bureau chief Larry Collins, about General Pierre Gallois' defection, and wanted to know where we had gotten the story. It apparently paralleled a secret cable from Paris, and Kennedy suspected that someone at the State Department had leaked it to us, despite the Paris dateline. I told him I knew it came from Paris, because I had been asked to check the story from here.

"You wouldn't shit me, would you?" he asked with a smile.

Part Four   THE DOMESTIC SCENE

Chapter 13 KENNEDY'S EGGHEADS

GARY WILLS (b. 1934) has been Henry
Luce professor of American Culture and Public Policy at Northwestern University since
1980. Among his many books is *The Kennedy
Imprisonment*, a sharply critical analysis of all
things Kennedy. In this excerpt he discusses
style and culture in the New Frontier. What
exactly does Wills mean by asserting that the
President "subverted" his most intellectual
advisers?

Washington positively fizzed in 1961. Kennedy had assembled a cabinet of all the
talents. Brilliant people circulated, telling each other how brilliant they were. As
Arthur Schlesinger remembers it:

> Washington seemed engaged in a collective effort to make itself brighter, gayer,
> more intellectual, more resolute. It was a golden interlude. . . . One's life seemed
> almost to pass in review as one encountered Harvard classmates, wartime associ-
> ates, faces seen after the war in ADA conventions, workers in Stevenson cam-
> paigns, academic colleagues, all united in a surge of hope and possibility.

Both Schlesinger and Sorensen proudly count up the Rhodes Scholars riding the New
Frontier.

From *The Kennedy Imprisonment: A Meditation On Power*, copyright 1981. Reprinted by permission of
Little, Brown, & Co. Inc., & Scott Meredith Literary Agency.

These "eggheads" boasted of their worldliness. Harvard professors, moving south, shed weight and wives, changed eyeglasses for contact lenses, worked hard and played hard. Schlesinger delights in the fact that Kenneth Galbraith not only wrote economic tomes but satiric essays in *Esquire* (Schlesinger was writing movie reviews for *Show* while serving in the White House). In describing Richard Goodwin as "the archetypal New Frontiersman," Schlesinger includes among his credentials "dining with Jean Seberg." Sorensen gives the President's friendship with Frank Sinatra as proof of his "range." The crush of intellectuals around Marilyn Monroe, at the President's birthday party, became a favorite memory. . . .

Harvard's urge toward Washington was so intense that it carried the professors halfway to Hollywood. At the Kennedy Library, the symbol of White House culture is the legendary night Pablo Casals played in the East Room. But Kennedy himself showed more interest in the planning and performances of his own birthday salutes— the first in Madison Square Garden, the second in Washington's National Guard Armory. Richard Adler, who wrote the musicals *Pajama Game* and *Damn Yankees*, was "master of revels" at these parties. For the first one, Adler brought in Marilyn Monroe to croon happy birthday for the President. And he topped himself the next year:

> I directed operations from the balcony through phones to the lighting and sound men, the conductor in the pit and the stage manager backstage. Everybody was in the Armory, waiting. And when the President made his entrance and began to walk to the Presidential box, I pinned him with a spot and cued six trumpets for "Ruffles and Flourishes." You know: "Tum-ta-ta, tum-ta-ta, tum-ta-ta." I tell you, it was terrific! A Roman emperor entering the Colosseum wouldn't have been more dramatic! Such a roar went up from the crowd. And right away we went into "Hail to the Chief." It was fantastic! Then we give the press boys one and a half minutes for pictures, they like it, and also it adds to the excitement. Meanwhile we are lowering the lights, and I have a drum roll going, and as each group of lights goes out and the drums get louder and louder until finally they are very loud, and at that point I have two flags up high above the stage, and there are fans behind them, and the flags are picked up by spots and they billow out and I had a great singer, John Reardon, to sing the National Anthem, which is usually dull in a show. Well, I want to say that the minute the National Anthem started and those flags lit up, the crowd was on its feet, applauding (did you ever see that before?), and after Reardon finished singing he took a bow, which nobody has ever done before, and they gave him a wonderful reception. . . . We never had a President like this.

Mr. Adler knew how to please his patron: "This was the President's party, not one of those culture-vulture programs." It was a giddy time. Remembering an early White House party for the Radziwills, Schlesinger writes in *A Thousand Days*: "Never had girls seemed so pretty, tunes so melodious, an evening so blithe and unconstrained."

Even international fashions seemed to resonate to the anglophile and "swinging" tastes of Kennedy. Mary Quant's London became the center of "the action," and Americans itched outward to Petula Clark's "rhythms of the gentle bossa nova." Schlesinger raved in *Show* about Julie Christie, Peter Sellers, and (of course) the Beatles: "They are the timeless essences of the adolescent effort to deal with the absurdities of an adult world." *Real* culture was not safe, not dull and respectable like Eisenhower's early-to-bed shows. It was frisky, and risqué.

Yet elegant, too: "In an Executive Mansion where Fred Waring once flourished, one now finds Isaac Stern, Pablo Casals, and the Stratford Players," Schlesinger assured us. Mrs. Kennedy—whose next husband would decorate in whale testicles—became the very embodiment of Culture. For the best and the brightest, attracted to her husband, she personified all that was most beautiful. She defied the rule that political wives must wear American clothes and drink American wines. But that, too, separated her husband's White House from the Fred Waring days. Schlesinger approved:

> The things people had once held against her—the unconventional beauty, the un-American elegance, a taste for French clothes and French food—were suddenly no longer liabilities but assets. She represented all at once not a negation of her country but a possible fulfillment of it, a dream of civilization and beauty, a suggestion that America was not to be trapped forever in the bourgeois deal.

So glittering did the Kennedy style appear that some accused the President of being all style, no substance. Schlesinger answered that such style was itself a political act of substantial import: "His 'coolness' was itself a new frontier. It meant freedom from the stereotyped response of the past. . . . His personality was the most potent instrument he had to awaken a national desire for something new and better." When one man's personality is an administration's most potent tool, then efficient use of resources dictates a cult of that personality. A shrewd administrator must, to achieve his policy goals, maximize the impact of the leader's charm—must, that is, join in the contriving of images to celebrate the prince. Honorary Kennedys had always tended the family image. Now an entire administration would be recruited to that task.

Sorensen's book tells us how carefully Kennedy crafted his symbols. When his back troubles forced him to use crutches, these signs of weakness were abandoned whenever he moved into an area of the White House where he could be seen. On the other hand, his rocking chair was an acceptable sign of relaxation. Even the chair had its carefully chosen "image," making it "a nationally recognized symbol of the traditional values, reflective patience, and practical informality prevailing in the White House." Hugh Sidey called Kennedy's chair "a symbol of him and his administration," with "the full status of F.D.R.'s cigarette holder."

The chair stood for relaxation, not weakness. The President declared the need for "vigah," and sent his "frontiersmen" off on fifty-mile hikes. He cut back on his own golfing, and avoided photographers when he did indulge the sport—he did not want to be compared with grandfatherly Eisenhower at this retirement sport. The putting green on the White House lawn, Ike's spike marks on the Oval Office floor, became objects of ridicule. Yet, away from the cameras, Kennedy drove golf balls toward the Washington Monument, and bet "Red" Fay he could not sent a drive over the Ellipse fence. . . .

Kennedy's task, according to his followers, was to combat the national enervation caused by Eisenhower. If the country had to get "moving again," it was because Eisenhower had brought it to such a total standstill. In this view, presidential style not only establishes an agenda for politics but determines the tone of national life. The image projected by the President becomes the country's self-image, sets the expectations to which it lives up and down. This was the reading of history that made style equal substance; and the Kennedy transition seemed to confirm the reading. If Kennedy could suddenly energize the press, the academy, and the arts, it was because Eisenhower had previously narcotized them. Only the vigor projected by a President can animate the citizenry. . . .

What, after all, in Ike's avuncular image automatically turned off thought? On the night he was elected, did his stealthy minions, some guardian angels of boredom, slip into newspaper rooms and faculty offices, to stuff invisible pillows in the typewriters? Did they proscribe the reading of philosophy? If so, how was the proscription enforced? Did a painter wake up, late one November morning in 1952, and decide he must pack his brushes away for at least four years? Conversely, did Kennedy's election make a philosopher wake up, look at his morning paper, and say, "At last I can start thinking again?"

Put this way, it seems an absurd claim. Yet that is what Schlesinger and others believed. The appearance of Pablo Casals in the White House became for them a signal that America had adopted art as a national purpose, even as part of the Cold War: "I would hope that we will not leave it to the Soviet Union to uncover the Van Cliburns of the future," Schlesinger wrote. Poor dumb Eisenhower—he not only lost Cuba; he lost Cliburn. He created the pianist gap.

What was the political meaning of Casals (rather than Waring) in the White House? It provided John Kennedy his first opportunity to hear the cellist—and late education is better than none; though there is no evidence that the evening made Kennedy give up his show tunes for Bach. Did Casals need the boost? Hardly. Some of the Harvard faculty types coming to Washington had, no doubt, listened to Casals before; those who had not were as little likely as Kennedy himself to become addicted after this one exposure. Did the "unwashed" make a run for Casals records? If they did, the fad can hardly have lasted very long. Those who listen to Casals because the President endured one night of him will soon, I would bet, backslide in Fred Waring's direction.

What was the result of that fabled night, then? The ones who got most benefit were those who has listened to Casals all along. He did not play better, after that, or Bach sound better; but these listeners felt better—felt bigger. They had been endorsed. Listening to Bach received a presidential seal of approval. The obverse of this is that these people felt smaller under Eisenhower. Their Bach did not have that extra ingredient which can make all the difference—the President was not noticing the listeners as they listened.

This view of things gives to the President a stunning power—to bestow or withhold pleasure in Bach. But he can do this only if those craving for presidential approval have debilitated themselves—have given a ridiculous importance to their own pose as Listeners. David Halberstam argues that "the best and the brightest" were self-corrupting in their confidence—in their assurance that rational gifts and expertise and toughness can set the world straight. But there was a deep sense of social and cultural inferiority under the tough outer whir of analysis and blur of activity. These best and the brightest felt intimidated by the suspicion that Americans consider art and culture "sissy stuff." Yet here was a war-hero President saying it was all right to listen to Bach, to like art and French wines. The embarrassing gush of gratitude for this largesse infects Schlesinger's and Sorensen's books as much as Manchester's. The gratitude is expressed with varying degrees of sophistication, but it is essentially the same in all three men.

Blessed with the approval of this macho President, the cultural monitors would prove that he was not mistaken, that they were not sissies, by taking on Kennedy's own worldly and fast-living air. They would wink at his secret parties in the White House and think that the proper underside of aristocratic graces. The results of this in policy were a "frontier" love of guerrilla boldness, a contempt for dithering Adlai Stevenson and courtly Dean Rusk and moralizing Chester Bowles. Style meant that the President—and those who now dressed like him and spoke like him—did not want to be bored. They talked in wisecracks; wrote witty verse at cabinet meetings; used the code of a superior set. According to Harris Wofford, this style forbade the raising of some questions, the expression of "square" inhibitions, of "preachy" concerns. Chester Bowles was resented for having been right about the Bay of Pigs; but he was exiled from the State Department, not because he was right, but because he was dull. It was every man's duty, around Kennedy, to sound brilliant.

The pursuit of style as if it were substance leaches vitality from the style itself. The Kennedy rhetoric sounds flashy now; raises snickers. This is not simply a matter of passing time and changing fashions. Dr. King's sermons retain their power to move us—but of course they were overtly preachy, moral and old-fashioned. Arthur Schlesinger hailed a cultural revolution, and gave up his monumental work on the Roosevelt years to suppress a report on the Bay of Pigs project at the *New Republic*, to mislead Adlai Stevenson during the missile crisis, to browbeat William Attwood at *Look*, and (in the words of Murray Kempton) "to fall upon William Manchester in the alleys of the American Historical Association." Kennedy did not liberate the intellectuals who praised him; he subverted them. He played to all that was weakest and worst in them. It became apparent that they did not simply want a President who praised them for listening to Bach; they wanted a President who would listen to them, and they were willing to say whatever "played" with him. National purpose would compensate for private failure, would fill with public rhetoric the empty places in them where poetry should have been breeding. Men rose up from the ruins of their family to redeem their country; or preached the comity of nations because they could not abide the members of their own university department.

Benefactors of mankind may start tending to the world, at least in part, to get out of the house. But artists and academicians, writers and the privileged journalists seem to feel a special responsibility for what goes on in Washington, a personal guilt when things go badly. They are prominent among those who make the threat that they will leave the country if so-and-so gets elected. This threat is not very terrifying, since its auditors would think it a blessing if fulfilled. And I do not personally know any intellectual who has missed a meal, or been put significantly off his feed, by the victory of an unpalatable candidate. But they undoubtedly think they should feel sad, and that the untoward election has blunted their creativity if not their appetite. One catches in faculty gossip about politicians the note of housewives wrapped up in soap operas—the note of a substitute vitality, shared artificial crises that alleviate the speaker's own problems. They may not agree on the merits of a "minimester," but they all hated Nixon. More important, they all agreed to love Prince Charming. We mainly spread havoc under Presidents we love. Camelot was the opium of the intellectuals.

Later, under the dreaded Nixon, celebrators of the New Frontier began to express misgivings about the Imperial Presidency. Schlesinger himself then traced the growth of presidential power, admitting faults in his heroes, Jackson and Roosevelt and Kennedy. But Kennedy's short time in office was not just an acceleration of prior trends. It added something new—not so much the Imperial Presidency as the Appearances Presidency. . . .

Kennedy was admired by liberals for his nonsentimental realism. He always said ADA types made him uncomfortable. He was "beyond ideology." This calculating approach thrilled the idealogues themselves. Schlesinger said it best: his coolness *was* a new frontier. But few intellectuals saw the contempt mixed with his coolness when it came to manipulating them. When Kennedy suggested that Walter Lippmann be offered an ambassadorship, Schlesinger replied that he might do the administration more good as a columnist. Kennedy worked always to turn journalists into unofficial spokesmen for his administration, and he succeeded with a great many of them. They were there to help him arrange reality, to make style become substance, to define power as the contriving of appearances.

But Kennedy could not have shaped his dazzling facade of style unless he had a genuine feel for many of its components. He liked the kind of glamour he was now in a position to dispense. The largely imaginary English society he had read about was his to "re-create," given all the resources of the White House. The very thinness of his grasp upon Regency England helped him enact a simulacrum of it, without regard for recalcitrant historical particulars. His imagined England was a world of playboy-statesmen, and America's more purchasable intellectuals wanted nothing better. They lined up to celebrate the second coming of a secondhand Lord Melbourne.

Chapter 14 THE DOMESTIC PROGRAMS

DAVID BURNER (b. 1937) is professor of
history at the State University of New York at
Stony Brook. Here he discusses the President's
domestic goals and activities. Why was Kennedy relatively ineffective with Congress?
What does his confrontation with Secretary
Celebrezze reveal?

The way for congressional legislation was cleared by Speaker of the House Sam
Rayburn on the last day of January 1961. The experienced Mr. Sam rammed through,
by a slim five-vote margin, the enlarging of the House Rules Committee so that it
could no longer bottle up liberal legislation. The president's vigorous state of the union
address the day before assured the nation that there would be new efforts in foreign
policy. But what about domestic needs? In that area the programs that Kennedy
presented to Congress were highly conventional extensions of the New Deal welfare
state: $5 billion for urban renewal housing projects, funds for retraining in areas of
high unemployment (the Manpower Development and Training Act of 1962), increased funds for treating water pollution, aid for businessmen who would locate in
depressed areas (the Area Redevelopment Bill of 1961), food stamps, an increased

minimum wage, an easing of eligibility for Social Security, the Peace Corps, greater mental health spending, a Cape Cod National Seashore, an Arms Control and Disaramament Agency, and Medicare. Except for Medicare all of these proposals became law under Kennedy. Perhaps he would have done more if Rayburn had lived beyond 1961 when he was replaced by the less effective John McCormack of Massachusetts. McCormack did not get along with the president and even teamed with Representative James Delaney of New York City and influential Republicans to bury Kennedy's attempt to keep more public funds from parochial schools. In the Senate the powerful Lyndon Johnson was succeeded as Democratic leader by the less effective Mike Mansfield. Without Rayburn or Johnson to help in Congress, the president alone had to coax support from conservative leaders like Senator Robert Kerr of Oklahoma, a slow and cumbersome process for which Kennedy sometimes lacked patience. Some Democrats, like Wilbur Mills of the Ways and Means Committee, even found the White House "timid."

Questions have been raised about how effective Kennedy's programs, embodying party policy advanced by Democrats in the 1950s, really were. Free market advocates have argued that raising the minimum wage eliminates jobs for the poor: employers would close down or substitute machines for workers. Perhaps so, but a submarginal wage for adults is an evasion of the modern welfare state's responsibilities. Area redevelopment, offering cheap federal loans to potential employers and providing grants to municipalities, is another favorite target of free market economists; they charge that excessive attention to families with deep attachments to their region threw money away in areas once thriving but since weakened by depletion of resources or shifts in markets. Few jobs, in fact, came out of the program, and most of the money went to Democratic congressional districts. Lyndon Johnson's well-funded poverty program, the Economic Opportunity Act of 1965, followed much the same guidelines with uncertain results. The Omnibus Housing Act of 1961, which appropriated $2 billion for urban renewal, often substituted middle-class housing on sites hitherto occupied by slums. Congenial ethnic neighborhoods with strong family bonds were often damaged in the process. But millions of families earning below a living wage also came to occupy the new buildings. The Manpower Development and Training Act, which was to retrain workers displaced by automation, merely retrained workers for other entry-level jobs. Without adequate basic education to start with, the trainees wound up only slightly better off than before. The one measure that might have helped such people, aid for education, was derailed because the bishops of the Catholic Church decided to kill it rather than be excluded from its benefits. Still, all the programs were at least susceptible to standard conservative criticisms: perversion by bureaucrats, both in Washington and in large cities; violation of market logic; and favoritism to special interests.

The measure that generated wide interest over the years was the Juvenile Delinquency and Youth Offenses Control Act of 1961. The agency it established was run by a childhood friend of Robert Kennedy, David Hackett, upon whom the novelist John

Knowles patterned the daring athlete-hero of *A Separate Peace*. All this appealed greatly to the president who believed physical training would maintain individual and national vigor, making "a nation of spectators" into a "nation of participants." Hackett, a sort of bureaucratic guerrilla, took charge of an entity called the President's Committee on Juvenile Delinquency, which never met formally. He recruited Lloyd Ohlin, research director of the Columbia School of Social Work, and his colleague Richard Piven to set up a series of Mobilization for Youth cadres in cities. The idea was to test whether, after having their expectations raised, slum kids could be enticed into legitimate opportunities for social advancement rather than turning to crime if they had no recourse to other avenues of success. Most cities created non-profit private corporations, bringing together social workers, college teachers, and private and public civic leaders to bypass the middle-class curricula of schools that shunned slum students and encouraged failure; the public welfare departments that robbed families of dignity and stability; and city government that provided services of poor quality except for police who acted as instruments of social control. Robert Kennedy in particular came to see the difference in the justice process for poor people versus those of stable means. He established within the Justice Department an Office for Criminal Justice to ensure free counsel for poor defendants. In 1963 the president introduced a proposed criminal justice act "to assure effective legal representation for every man." *The Other America*, Michael Harrington's stirring discovery of the poor, got through to the conscience of the Kennedys; the violence of black demonstrations made its separate argument for relieving poverty.

During the president's final months plans were being considered to make an antipoverty program the lynchpin of his 1964 campaign. During the 1960 contest the candidate had occasionally discussed poverty, once declaring that the "war against poverty" is not over. By 1963 the idea of fighting poverty with funds derived from a more expansive economy following a tax cut seemed politically eye-catching, and the president thought of dramatizing the issue by traveling through Appalachia. Most Southerners would not object to poverty funds since their region would benefit disproportionately. Actually, the administration envisioned only a several-hundred-million-dollar program. But it would be a coordinated assault, and the notion of poverty amid plenty would be the focus along with the social obligation of the rich to the poor. At Robert Kennedy's home, Hickory Hill, administration members fought it out. George Kennan said the poor would always be with us, but Robert Kennedy strenuously disagreed. On November 20, 1963, the president expressed reservations about concentrating on poverty alone in 1964 and thought something should be done for the middle class at the same time.

Action seemed remote. For one thing, Kennedy was occupied by a series of foreign policy crises far more wrenching than those of the Eisenhower years. He put domestic issues aside whenever he could. Secretary of Agriculture Orville Freeman has said the president was "restless and uncomfortable" when talking about farm issues. When Secretary of Health, Education, and Welfare Anthony Celebrezze tried to speak to him about new legislation, Kennedy told him to go away: "You were the mayor of a large city. You know how to handle these problems. Now handle them." Celebrezze did, holding a famous press conference that focused on the relationship between smoking cigarettes and cancer (during which he chain-smoked). Nor did the makeup of Congress invite bold legislation. Of the 261 Democrats in the House, 101 were Southerners, most of them conservatives. The new president did put his prestige on the line to enlarge the size of the House Rules Committee, where much important liberal legislation had previously been bottled up, but he won this contest so narrowly that he had little taste for more combat with Congress. The *Kiplinger Washington Letter* correctly predicted that Kennedy would "*step around*" domestic problems, waiting for better Democratic majorities.

Chapter 15 PROSPERITY AND THE NEW FRONTIER

BRUCE MIROFF (b. 1945) is associate professor of political science at the State University of New York at Albany. His *Pragmatic
Illusions, The Presidential Politics Of John F.
Kennedy* is a left-wing critique of the New
Frontier. In this excerpt, Miroff analyzes the
prosperity Americans enjoyed during the Kennedy years. Is this inequality of income he
documents the deliberate result of Administration policy? Are "pragmatic liberals" always
subservient to Big Business?

Much of President Kennedy's stature in the field of economic policy rests upon the tax
cut enacted several months after his death, and the continued economic expansion
which extended several years into the term of his successor. . . .

Kennedy's 1960 campaign pledge to lift America's rate of economic growth up to
the 5 percent mark had been fulfilled even before the tax cut was passed early in 1964.
From the first quarter of 1961 to the fourth quarter of 1963, the average annual increase
in GNP had been 5.4 percent. Thanks largely to tax reduction, even higher figures
were obtained during the first two years of the Johnson Administration, with the rise in
GNP exceeding 6 percent. Until the escalation of the Vietnam War imposed fresh and
unexpected strains upon the Kennedy-Johnson fiscal policy, that policy was respons-

ible for the longest recorded period of peacetime economic expansion in the nation's history.

Kennedy had promised to enlarge the American economic pie; measurably he succeeded. The Kennedy years and the first few Johnson years were a time of prosperity, a period in which the standard of living was demonstrably improving for most Americans. The sluggishness of the Eisenhower years had given way to economic vigor. In place of widespread economic anxiety there was a pervasive optimism. Looked at these broad terms, Kennedy's economic accomplishments are impressive, and his policy must be accounted a success.

Nevertheless, it is important to ask a question that Kennedy and his economic advisers preferred not to ask; How were the benefits of this new prosperity distributed? If the majority of Americans gained from this economic expansion, what classes or groups gained the most? Here, by comparing the statistics on corporate profits with those on employee compensation and unemployment, a rather different picture of Kennedy-Johnson fiscal policy emerges.

First, let us consider the years 1961–63, before Kennedy tax cut took effect. How did corporate stockholders (including most of management), employed workers, and the unemployed fare in these years? Corporate profits in this period jumped a spectacular 44 percent before taxes—and 52 percent after taxes, thanks to the tax breaks of 1962. Employee compensation, adjusted for the mild rise in consumer prices, rose only 7 percent in three years; here the effects of the wage guidelines were especially perceptible. Unemployment dropped from 6.7 percent during the 1960–61 recession to 5.6 percent in 1962, but remained near that relatively high figure throughout 1963.

The record for workers and the unemployed was somewhat better in the years 1964–65, a period during which the effects of the tax cut were felt. In 1965, for example, weekly earnings for employees went up 3.5 percent. And on these higher wages they were paying their federal income taxes at a reduced rate. The unemployment situation was dramatically improved; the rate of unemployment stood at only 4.1 percent in December of 1965. As for corporate profits, they continued to skyrocket; for 1965 alone, profits were up 15 percent before taxes, 20 percent after taxes.

The story that these statistics tell is summed up in the figures for the "distribution of gross product originating in nonfinancial corporations." The share of gross product taken by the employees of these corporations as compensation fell each year, from 65.1 percent in 1961 to 62.6 percent in 1965. The share of gross product that went for profits mounted each year, from 14.5 percent in 1961 to 17.0 percent in 1965.

Economic growth policies during the Kennedy-Johnson Administrations were designed to benefit all Americans—and generally they did so. But, as the above statistics indicate, they benefited the prosperous far more than they did people of low or moderate income. The wealthy already owned a disproportionate slice of the American economic pie. From Kennedy's enlargements to the pie, they again received a disproportionate share. Kennedy's impressive record on economic growth hence must be balanced by his record on economic distribution and equity. That record, if judged in terms of Kennedy's expressed sympathies for the underdogs in American society, can only be deemed a sorry one.

The economic stature of the Kennedy Administration does not, however, rest solely upon impressive growth figures. Equally important with the prosperity Kennedy's Presidency produced, his admirers argue, are the methods by which that prosperity was produced. Those methods—devised by Lord Keynes and refined by several generations of American economists—owed little to Kennedy for their formulation; but his sponsorship won them mass acceptance and finally enshrined them as official federal policy. In the eyes of his admirers, the Kennedy years were, thereby, a watershed in American economic history. [Kennedy Treasury Secretary Douglas Dillon observed:]

> They have borne witness to the emergence, first of all, of a new national determination to use fiscal policy as a dynamic and affirmative agent in fostering economic growth. Those years have also demonstrated, not in theory, but in actual practice, how our different instruments of economic policy—expenditure, tax, debt management and monetary policies—can be tuned in concert toward achieving different, even disparate, economic goals. In short, those years have encompassed perhaps our most significant advance in decades in the task of forging flexible economic techniques capable of meeting the needs of our rapidly changing economic scene.

It could be argued that this "Keynesian Revolution" (as some of Kennedy's admirers have called it) was so vital to the nation's economic health that it justified a skewing of rewards in the direction of the prosperous. The continuation, and even intensification, of economic inequality was a price that had to be paid—along with such short-term sacrifices as abandonment of tax reform and a freeze upon welfare spending—in order to modernize American fiscal policy. This argument appears persuasive, as long as it is assumed that the "Keynesian Revolution" has been an unmixed blessing. Yet it is possible to view that "revolution," at least in the form in which it was carried through by Kennedy, as of ambiguous value.

Certainly Kennedy's economic achievements represented an advance over his predecessors. The tenets of modern Keynesian theory were, under his aegis, substituted for the hidebound maxims of economic orthodoxy. Flexible tools were developed to improve the federal government's management of the economy, to combat its periodic failures and extend its surges of expansion. The government— to be precise, the President—emerged from Kennedy's "Keynesian Revolution" in a stronger, and more widely accepted, position as director of the American economy than ever before.

Yet all this hardly constituted an economic "revolution" (a word used, as we have already seen in the case of the Alliance for Progress, rather loosely on the New Frontier). The New Frontiersmen's excitement over what was essentially an advance in techniques diverted their attention from the fundamentally conservative impact of those techniques. A parallel might be drawn here with the counterinsurgency fad. The New Frontiersmen were enthused by the prospect of intervening in social and economic processes with sophisticated new techniques. They failed to heed the fact that those techniques assumed the maintenance of established structures of power.

The sector of the American economy that Kennedy's "New Economics" techniques served best was big business. His innovations were, in the last analysis, not a threat, but a prop to the established economic hierarchy. And this conclusion—however unpalatable it might seem to the liberal architects of the "New Economics"—was one which even the conservative business community was finally to draw.

Perhaps the most striking feature of Kennedy's "Keynesian Revolution" was the rapidity with which it became the new orthodoxy. Sophisticated leaders of the corporate world had endorsed Kennedy's tax reduction plans from the outset. Once the tax cut actually took effect in 1964, almost the entire business community began to embrace this brand of Keynesian fiscal policy. In the sober language of *Business Week*, "the lesson of 1964 is that fiscal policy needs to be used actively and steadily if balanced long-term growth is to be achieved."

As corporate profits soared, and executive salaries were padded by tax reduction and higher stock dividends, remaining business suspicions of Kennedy's economic program evaporated—particularly since it was now in the hands of the reassuring Lyndon Johnson. Businessmen, Robert Lekachman observed, were at last discovering "that economic expansion was assisted by the termination of the traditional civil war between Democratic national administrations and the business community." The "end of ideology" which Kennedy had called for a Yale had seemingly come. "Business recognition that prudent Keynesian fiscal policies promote larger markets and higher profits had had an unexpected effect. Keynesian prescriptions, the monopoly of reformers and radicals during the 1930's and the 1940's, have very nearly become the favorite medicines of the established, propertied interests in the community."

The alliance between government and business which Kennedy had so earnestly pursued thus became firm, reflecting a convergence on economic philosophy as well as a growing recognition of congruent interests. In the next few years this alliance appeared as part of the Johnsonian consensus, its special nature and importance partially obscured by the other linkages within that consensus. And just as in the Kennedy years—when, in spite of its animosity toward the federal government, the business community received a greater largesse than Kennedy's political supporters—the principal beneficiary of Johnson's consensus was, once more, business. . . .

Kennedy-Johnson fiscal policy can, in short, best be characterized as "conservative expansionism." While corporate power and profits were blooming throughout the 1960s, social needs continued to go unfulfilled. Despite President Johnson's rhetorical extravagance regarding a "War on Poverty" and a "Great Society," the inadequacy of social services—which John Kenneth Galbraith had vividly underscored during the original debate over the tax cut—was scarcely alleviated by the time Johnson left office.

Once it lost its air of controversy for an increasingly sophisticated business community, the "New Economics" settled into an ongoing process of economic tinkering which substituted for—and in large part foreclosed—genuine economic and social change. It had some notable successes in the mid-1960s—and some important failures later on, as the problems of maintaining economic expansion with full employment and stable prices proved more complicated than they had earlier appeared. Never did it seriously concern itself with the problem of inequity in the American economy. Nor did it ever confront the enormity of corporate power. The triumphs of pragmatic liberalism in the field of economic policy thus masked a deeper failure, a failure to address the fundamental deficiencies in American economic life. Those liberal triumphs had, it is true, won over many conservatives—but only at the cost of ensuring that the conservative, corporate definition of the American economy, now decked out in sophisticated Keynesian dress, remained ascendant.

Chapter 16 THE ISSUE OF RACE

Since 1982, historian CARL M. BRAUER (b. 1945) has been with the Institute of Politics at the John F. Kennedy School of Government, Harvard University. In this selection, Brauer attempts to "draw up a balance sheet of Kennedy's civil rights record." How much of the President's activities stemmed from political considerations? How seriously did Kennedy effect the course of the civil rights movement?

In the quarter century before Kennedy became President, his predecessors initiated a number of measures to advance civil rights, but Kennedy's activism in this regard far surpassed any of theirs. Franklin D. Roosevelt tolerated civil rights advocacy among his lieutenants, although he cautiously refrained from using the Presidency or his own enormous personal prestige to promote equal treatment of blacks. Under considerable pressure from militant blacks on the eve of American entrance into World War II, Roosevelt created the Fair Employment Practices Commission, but invested it with meager enforcement powers. Harry S. Truman pioneered in the employment of Presidential power on behalf of racial progress, ordering the desegregation of the military, speaking out against the ill-treatment of blacks, and creating a blue-ribbon committee on civil rights. Overall, however, civil rights played a relatively minor role in his administration, with issues of foreign policy, the economy, and internal security predominating. An uncooperative Congress, meanwhile, blocked his legislative recommendations on civil rights. Dwight D. Eisenhower proceeded down the trails of executive action Truman had blazed, but displayed little enthusiasm for the task. His heart never belonged to the civil rights cause, and Eisenhower generally played a passive role in the gains that did occur during his Presidency, including the Brown decision and its follow-up, and the enactment of civil rights legislation in 1957 and 1960. Kennedy, by contrast, turned Truman's trails into wide avenues. He used his executive powers broadly, promoting an end to racial discrimination in voting, schools, the federal government, jobs, public facilities, and housing. He committed the moral authority of the President to racial justice in the most clear-cut terms ever. And he proposed and made significant progress toward securing the most important piece of civil rights legislation in a century. Under Kennedy civil rights became a focal point of public policy and political debate. Moreover, so unambiguous had Kennedy's commitment to civil rights been that it is hard to imagine any Vice President who succeeded him in November 1963, reversing it.

Kennedy's motives for proceeding as he did on the civil rights issue were complex, but for the sake of understanding may be divided into three types: political, attitudinal or intellectual, and personal. Naturally his actions at different times derived from different combinations of these and to different degrees. For example, politics dominated during the 1960 campaign, but when the Birmingham crisis erupted, factors of attitude and personality were most important. In addition, each kind of motive changed intrinsically over time; his political needs as a newly elected President, for instance, differed somewhat from the requirements of candidacy. Likewise his view of Reconstruction underwent a significant change. Looking briefly at each of these motives in isolation helps clarify Kennedy's actions and effects.

Kennedy was a consummate politician. As a Senator ambitious for the Presidency, he carried the favor of civil rights proponents and opponents. In the end he succeeded in winning critical support from both sides without trading away basic principle. He promised new Presidential leadership but assured the white South that he would not be vindictive. Once elected, he had to contend with a Congress in which the Southern wing of his party possessed disproportionate power. Consequently, he did not immediately carry through on his promise of civil rights legislation and compromised on his executive action program. Nevertheless, that program marked a significant break with the past, achieved some meaningful results, and perhaps most important, raised the hopes of black people. Indeed, higher black expectations led ultimately to Kennedy's changing his approach in June 1963. The task of getting his proposed legislation enacted in turn presented a challenge to his political leadership, which he rose to meet. He rallied important segments of the public to his cause, and in time won several key Congressional skirmishes. Simultaneously, as a candidate for reelection, he began to mend his Southern fences preparatory to his next and expectedly last campaign. To the end, he neither abandoned nor excoriated the white South. Black voters, it appeared, had meanwhile given him nearly complete allegiance.

Certain ideas guided Kennedy. As an American nationalist, he was troubled by the damage racial intolerance was inflicting upon his country's image abroad, particularly in the Third World where he hoped to expand American influence. As a student of American history, on the other hand, he for a long time accepted a simplistic though widely held view of Reconstruction as a vindictive reign of terror and corruption which the North had visited upon the South. This perspective helped smooth his relations with Southern officeholders. Eventually, confrontations with ardent segregationists led him to question his former assumptions about the first Reconstruction and eased the way toward his launching a second, though he never advocated punishing the region. In addition, Kennedy worried about the damaging effects racial discrimination had on the nation's economy and on the health and education of its citizens. He shared the modern liberal's faith that the central government, led by an active President, could and should solve pressing social problems, of which racial discrimination was a leading one. Finally, Kennedy believed that all citizens should receive the same treatment regardless of race. Racial discrimination offended him intellectually. Hence, he shared with the civil rights movement a fundamental belief.

Personal factors also shaped Kennedy's handling of civil rights. His grace and style charmed black delegates in personal meetings. Sensitivity and empathy contributed to his making symbolic gestures of signifiance, such as calling Coretta King, and permitted him to comprehend, on more than an intellectual level, the struggle for equal rights. Finally, Kennedy needed to feel that he was leading rather than being swept along by events. As President, he was uncomfortable playing a passive role. Therefore, when in the spring of 1963 he perceived that he was losing the reins of leadership, he boldly reached out to grasp them once again.

Kennedy's exercise of leadership probably helped instill in many potential civil rights activists a confidence and daring that they would not otherwise have had. In this regard it might be recalled that James Meredith applied to Ole Miss the day Kennedy was inaugurated and that for Anne Moody, Kennedy had made " 'Real Freedom' a hope." Indeed, the spirit Kennedy conveyed may well have made possible the eruption of social protest to which he in turn responded. Certainly Kennedy did not create the civil rights movement, but he did affect its course. Some of the things that occurred during his years as President probably would have occurred in any case. Most definitely the Freedom Rides would have taken place and undoubtedly there would have been some other direct challenges to segregation. But what would have happened had Richard Nixon been elected President? Would he have sent marshals to Montgomery, would a Voter Education Project have been created, would the Justice Department have dramatically stepped up enforcement under the guidance of someone like Robert Kennedy, would thousands of blacks have demonstrated in Birmingham, and, most important, if they had, would Nixon have responded by proposing and working for enactment of sweeping civil rights legislation?

Those conservative critics who in 1963 charged Kennedy with encouraging massive law-breaking were in a sense not so wide of the mark. Kennedy, of course, never urged blacks to march in the streets, but he did foster an atmosphere where protests against the status quo could occur. He created that atmosphere through symbolic acts such as phoning Coretta King, appointing Thurgood Marshall to the federal bench, and opening the White House to blacks, and through more substantive deeds such as establishing a close working relationship between the Justice Department and the civil rights movement, sending marshals to Montgomery and Oxford, and using the executive powers of his office to combat discrimination. He also contributed to it in a general way, for in his campaign and in office, he represented change, not continuity; the future, not the past.

One could well draw up a balance sheet of Kennedy's civil rights record. On the minus side, one might list the appointment of segregationist judges in the South, the delay in the housing order followed by the promulgation of the narrowest possible one, as well as numerous instances of executive cautiousness. Kennedy could be faulted for not making even more high-level appointments of blacks than he did, especially to the White House staff, and for failing to remove barriers to effective criminal enforcement that existed within the federal government, specifically within the FBI. One might also want to add the fact that Kennedy did not win enactment of his proposed legislation. Yet, to blame the murdered Kennedy for that implies a callousness.

The plus side of the ledger would be considerably longer. It would include a large number of executive actions, such as the appointment of blacks to high offices and the gains in federal employment generally. In the upper civil service ranks, black employment increased 88 percent from June 1961 to June 1963, as compared to an overall increase at these levels of under 23 percent. High on the list would belong the many accomplishments relating to law enforcement, including the use of marshals to prevent mob rule in Montgomery, the application of legal pressure to bring about desegregation of transportation terminals, and the persistent implementation of court orders to effect desegregation at the universities of Mississippi and Alabama. Between Robert Kennedy's swearing in and his resignation in the summer of 1964, the number of voting rights suits increased from ten to sixty-nine, including statewide cases in Mississippi and Louisiana. The administration also scored some gains by promoting voluntary action. For example, partly as a result of Justice Department efforts, between May and December 1963, some voluntary desegregation of public accommodations took place in 356 out of 566 cities in the South and border states; biracial committees were established in at least 185 of these cities. Because the administration played a role in the creation of the Voter Education Project, it might be afforded partial credit for its accomplishments. By April 1964, the VEP had registered nearly 580,000 new voters in the South. President Kennedy's proposal of a broad civil rights bill in 1963 and his preliminary successes in getting that bill through Congress would also deserve places on the plus side of the ledger. Finally, Kennedy's exercise of moral leadership, through rhetorical advocacy and through personal example, would certainly merit inclusion in the positive column.

A balance sheet does not convey Kennedy's full importance, however. Kennedy was significant not only for what he did, but for what he started. His Presidency marked a profound change from the inertia that had generally characterized the past. In a tragically foreshortened term of less than three years, he instituted a vigorous and far-reaching effort to eliminate racial discrimination in American life. Operating within the bounds of a democratic political system, Kennedy both encouraged and responded to black aspirations and led the nation into its Second Reconstruction.

Part Five

THE FOREIGN POLICY

Chapter 17 COLD WAR LIBERALISM

THOMAS R. WEST (b. 1936) is associate
professor of history at The Catholic University
of America. In 1984, he and David Burner
(q.v.) co-authored *The Torch is Passed*, a sympathetic study of the Kennedys and American
liberalism. Here the historians discuss JFK's
basic thoughts about foreign policy, the Bays
of Pigs, and the Alliance for Progress. What
was "the political thinking of cold war liberalism"?

John Kennedy was a foreign policy president. It has been common for the presidency
in this century to receive much of its definition from the global events that impinge so
dramatically upon it. Kennedy, even among recent Presidents, has been distinctive in
the degree of his identification with those events. . . .

The "torch has been passed to a new generation of American, born in this century,
tempered by war, disciplined by a hard and bitter peace"—so go the famous words of
the inaugural at the transfer of power from the oldest elected President in the nation's
history to the youngest. The new generation, or much of it, had served under
Eisenhower or MacArthur in a war. The claim is now familiar that the war had
schooled the Kennedy people, made them quick to react to crisis, impatient with
bureaucracy, swift to improvise. After victory in 1945 it must have seemed to the war

generation that the world's ills would yield to the competent marshalling of power, and that the United States, the most powerful victor of the war, had the ability and the obligation to shape events. There was another side to the thought of this generation. Ellis Stair, secretary of the army under Kennedy, reports that the President wished that every military officer would read *The Guns of August*, Barbara Tuchman's account of the world that stumbled into war in 1914. "It is a dangerous illusion," he said at Berkeley on March 23, 1962, "to believe that the policies of the United States, stretching as they do worldwide, under varying and different conditions, can be encompassed in one slogan or one adjective, hard or soft or otherwise." It was a "simple central theme of American foreign policy," Kennedy once said, "to support the independence of nations so that one bloc cannot gain sufficient power to finally overcome us." John Gaddis in *Strategies of Containment* calls this "the most precise public explanation by an American president of what all postwar chief executives had believed, but rarely stated: that the American interest was not to remake the world but to balance power within." This belief has activist implications if the balancing is carried out in the Kennedy manner, by an incessant watchfulness, an infusing of military or economic aid to one region, an encouragement of progressive reform in another, a neutralization of dangerous conflict, as in Laos, a development of a swift and versatile military, and the sending forth of a skilled force of Peace Corps volunteers. A world to be balanced and rebalanced, indeed, invites an activity more extensive and exact than a world to be remade once and for all.

"In general," writes the journalist Carey McWilliams, "the liberals Kennedy attracted to Washington were more aggressively anti-Communist than the bureaucrats they replaced." But their anticommunism sought more sophisticated expression than Washington had previously employed. In wanting to renovate the military so that it would be a defter instrument for use in a complex power politics, Kennedy was taking the same position that Generals Maxwell Taylor and Matthew Ridgeway had earlier expounded in the Pentagon against the view that we should rely primarily on the nuclear deterrent. The United States, said Taylor, should be able to fight two wars and a half at once. Having retired in 1959, subsequently becoming president of the new Lincoln Center for the Performing Arts, Taylor returned in 1961 as an important presidential adviser. Taylor was a liberal's general. A scholar who could speak several languages, he argues in the *The Uncertain Trumpet* against founding national policy simplistically on the threat to use nuclear weapons. During the Berlin crisis of 1961 he was free enough of chauvinism to be able to say, in a note of July 7 to Secretary of State Dean Rusk, that it was not our rights in Berlin but our responsibilities to the West Berliners that mattered. A combination of the warrior, the seasoned critic of force, and the technician in Taylor favored tactical over strategic nuclear weapons, for the incorrect reason that they would produce virtually no fallout or danger to civilians. The Robert McNamaras of the administration, no spokesmen for the rhetoric that equated internal subversion with Soviet troops and negotiation with surrender, were given to the new militancy of surgical antiguerrilla tactics.

The counterfeit strategy soon announced by the administration, the plan to prepare our missiles for strikes not at enemy cities but at missile bases, was equally expressive of the technocrat liberal mind. It trusted in the precision of which missile technology is capable, it was supposed to allow for greater flexibility of action, and McNamara apparently sincerely preferred it as more humane than a policy aiming weapons at civilians. In July 1962 Kennedy and McNamara finally equipped overseas nuclear missiles with electronic locks so that their crews could not fire them without information from the government. Advances in missile construction decreed the eventual use of the device, but it was fitting to an administration that looked to technology for power and for the restraint of power. . . .

Some of the new administration's mentality quickly revealed itself at the Bay of Pigs. In the Eisenhower years, the Central Intelligence Agency had prepared an invasion force that it believed would bring a Cuban uprising against Fidel Castro. Cuban refugee guerrillas awaited orders on a coffee plantation in a mountainous region of Guatemala. In the campaign debates, Kennedy had come out of the hard-liner on Cuba, implicitly holding the Eisenhower administration responsible for letting Cuba go Communist, while Nixon, the liberal Republican, observed that we were obliged to work within the Organization of American States. Conservative columnists praised Kennedy; liberal commentators lauded Nixon, somewhat inaccurately, for the Vice President knew of the plans for invasion. So Kennedy as President had to make a decision about a scheme that his opponent had needed to shroud with soft language. Several liberals dissented from the plan. Arthur Schlesinger and William Fulbright voiced their objections to the President. Others did not get to make their case: Chester Bowles, intelligence expert Roger Hilsman of the Department of State, and George Kennen, the intellectual architect of the policy of containment. Another set of advisers got through to Kennedy.

Notable among these were the Joint Chiefs of Staff, including Arleigh Burke, the legendary navy chief, whom Kennedy admired. As Kennedy would soon discover, all the chiefs had a habit of favoring belligerent operations. Allen Dulles told him that probability of success for the act was higher than could have been predicted of the Eisenhower administration's successful intervention of 1954 in Guatemala. In April 1961 Kennedy gave the order for the assault on Cuba.

The landing spot, surrounded by swamps and allowing the rebels no opportunity to retreat to the mountains, was familiar in detail to Castro, for it was his favorite fishing spot. Maps studied for the invasion had little grasslike figures that one CIA participant could recognize as symbols for swamps. The other planners apparently did not possess the useful art of map reading and so could not see that the exiles would be pinched in. "I don't think we fully realized," writes Schlesinger, "that the Escambray Mountains lay *eighty miles* from the Bay of Pigs, across a hopeless tangle of swamps and jungles." He has also noted that one road believed to be important ended in a swamp. The force of 1,400 was challenging an army of 250,000 to 400,000, powerfully equipped by the Soviet Union. The invaders, using old freighters supplied by the

United Fruit Company, carried radio equipment and much of their inadequate supply of munitions in a single boat, which was blown up; air cover by the exiles was inadequate. Coral reefs ripped the hulls of some craft. In its spirit the enterprise recalls some of Kennedy's moments in World War II. Yet the President had the restraint not to provide major United States air support. Or perhaps it was not self-restraint but, as Senator George Smathers of Florida has reported Kennedy's telling him, Adlai Stevenson's threat to resign from the Ambassadorship to the United Nations. Another possible reason for Kennedy's forbearance was a message from Khrushchev that in the event of a more direct intervention the Soviet Union would take action—perhaps it would be in Berlin or Southeast Asia: "Cuba is not alone," Khrushchev announced. Kennedy's indefatigable champion Schlesinger was later to tell Robert Estabrook that while Eisenhower had contemplated American air and sea support and even American ground forces in a strike against the island, Kennedy had rejected that idea in March, before the invasion. Castro, in any event, destroyed the assault.

Just after the Bay of Pigs an analogy appeared several times in the press between the Russian invasion of Hungary in 1956, intended to protect the Soviet Union's sphere of influence, and the attempt on the part of the United States government to preserve its own international domain. As an exercise in realpolitik, the invasion was comparable. It would have been morally comparable only if the Soviets, instead of sending their own troops to kill thousands of Hungarians in order to crush a movement unpleasing to them, had sent in an army of Hungarian exiles, expecting them to rally the people in a coup against a repressive government. In 1961 the Cuban regime had more people in prison than the rightist former government had confined for an equal period, and the treatment of political prisoners was often brutal. Not only former supporters of Batista but anyone at whom the new order took political offense became a victim of the mass trials and mass executions of the early days of the Castro regime. Kennedy was acting on one of the most generous, and most naive, of American cold war beliefs. He assumed, in effect, that every people in the world wishes to be free in the way that the Western democracies understand freedom: with elected parliaments, a diverse and argumentative press, competing political parties, and a citizenry that conducts itself not by neighborhood committees ruthlessly enforcing ideological orthodoxy but by private choices. It may be that Cuba under Castro is free in ways that it was not before: free from extremes of hunger, disease, illiteracy; free to participate in local forms of self-management. The freedoms that Cubans do enjoy, if freedom is the right word, must be preferable to a life of malnutrition and sickness under governments that provide a measure of democratic debate for classes prosperous enough to relish or profit from it. Yet the beliefs that led legions of Americans to expect that nations would be content with nothing less than constitutional, parliamentary, civil libertarian freedom expressed the pride of the West in some of its finest political achievements of recent centuries. Kennedy would have had no patience with the species of radicalism that dismisses the liberties of the Western republics as merely bourgeois. . . .

If the expectations that led to the Bay of Pigs reveal the political thinking of cold war liberalism, they also demonstrate a liberal's, and a Kennedy's, faith in expertise. The Central Intelligence Agency, founded under President Truman in 1947, had been an outgrowth of the Office of Strategic Services, the American spy organization of World War II staffed with many scholars and often thought to lean leftward. In its own way the CIA was a liberal's institution, with its cluster of scholars and analysts of the sort who have historically staffed twentieth-century liberalism. During the Eisenhower and the Kennedy years, it is estimated, at least 10 percent of the agency's members held PhDs. . . .

CIA people, having turned their intellects outward from scholarship to the virile business of counterinsurgency, had nothing about them of the pallid, introspective hesitancy that a Kennedy despised in liberalism. The most enthusiastic of the experts who designed the Bay of Pigs was Richard Bissell, impatiently brilliant, eccentric, a former economics professor, a sailor and a mountain climber who appealed to the egotist in Kennedy. Bissell in an interview about a year after the attempt said that he had favored air support for the invaders, which he acknowledged could have brought a wider involvement. . . .

The Bay of Pigs turned Kennedy angry at the CIA and skeptical of officialdom. Some agency officers, in Robert's later description of them, had been disobedient, saying before the invasion that if the President were to call it off, they would arrange for the rebels to get American weapons—"virtually treason," in Robert's words. President Kennedy had insisted that no United States troops be used; the first two people on the beach were his countrymen, sent by the CIA. In the opinion of Robert, who after the disaster headed the program for building counterinsurgency forces, the Bay of Pigs may have been the best thing to happen to the administration, teaching his brother to trust only his own judgment and keeping the United States from a heavy commitment of troops to Laos. Here, in rough, is Robert's rendering, something of a parody, in an exchange between the President and the military eager to send troops to Laos. How would the troops get there? asked the President. Two airports could land them, he was told. How many could be landed? Under perfect conditions, came the response, a thousand a day. How many Communist troops would be in the area? At a guess, three thousand. How long, wondered the President, would it take the Communists to bring up four thousand? The answer: in four more days, five to eight thousand. What if we have landed three thousand on the third day and the Communists bomb the airport and concentrate five or six thousand more? Bomb Hanoi, was the military advice; use nuclear weapons. Chester Bowles has said that while Marine Corps Chief of Staff David Shoup could be reasonable on Laos, other chiefs wanted something major, such as air attacks on South China. Following the crisis of the Cuba missiles, Robert recounts, Navy Chief of Staff George Anderson, Jr., lamented, "We've been sold out," and Air Force Chief Curtis LeMay wanted to bomb Cuba anyway.

John Kennedy had remarked to Richard Neustadt at the beginning of his administration that he could not be a good President if he limited himself to one set of advisers. He did come to seek varieties of opinion, balancing Robert Kennedy and Sorensen, for example, against the military. The President, writes Adam Ulam, "became increasingly impressed by brilliantly reasoned, but not always realistic, academic theories and memoranda bearing on insurgency and nation-building." Upon the retirement of Allen Dulles from the directorship of the CIA, Kennedy appointed John McCone. The performance of the new director pleasantly startled liberals who had known him to be only a right-winger. Yet the incurable agency was still intruding on the administration as late as April 2, 1963, when Sargent Shriver called the President to ask that he restrain the CIA from planting people in the Peace Corps. Kennedy, the White House tapes record, agreed to do so. . . .

On military spending, too, Kennedy was acting like the hard-liner of the 1950s. Discounting the argument that building up our weaponry·would provoke the Soviet Union into a like program, the President pushed for greater funding for defense, and Congress passed a fifteen percent increase. The Russians did ultimately respond to our growth in weaponry as well as to the crisis of these years with their scheme for placing missiles in Cuba and with a long-term increase in their military expenditures. The obsession with Cuba has been one of the worst legacies of the Kennedy administration. Yet even in his belligerence the President, who during his campaign had said that we should "create a Latin America where freedom can flourish," adopted also the strategy of economic assistance that had reconciled the anticommunism of the liberals with their social progressivism.

Using the Bay of Pigs as a reason for acting, Kennedy pressed for an Alliance for Progress, a $10 billion decade-long program of economic aid to Latin America. At Punta del Este in Uruguay during 1962 the alliance committed itself to land and tax reform. Though the administration was never to carry its support for progressivism to the point of abandoning right-wing regimes that promised stability, the plan at its origins was assertively social reformist. Richard Goodwin, one of Kennedy's advisers, was instrumental in fashioning the alliance and worked to make it address political and social problems as well as economics. State Department officials had cooperated with rightist Latin American governments and were repelled when the President, in a speech of March 13, 1961, talked of "revolutionary ideas and efforts." The *alianza*, in Hilsman's words, "is saying a revolution is inevitable in Latin America. If you don't do it peacefully, you'll end up with blood." Juan Bosch, a progressive leader in the Dominican Republic whose politics Lyndon Johnson was to push aside with marines in 1965, has said of the Alliance, "That was the only time the U.S. ever followed a correct policy in Latin America."

Elsewhere as well the administration acted to the left of its defense spending. The Development Loan Fund in 1961 provided more than $1 billion in aid to underdeveloped nations. The administration united diverse foreign aid programs under the Agency for International Development. An objective of AID was counterinsurgency, but its plans for training local police in advanced technology were combined with progressive measures for emergency economic assistance to threatened areas and for technical aid for sanitation and transportation. Yet Congress in 1963, against Kennedy's wishes, sharply cut foreign aid in response to the recommendations of a conservative study group headed by General Lucius Clay that the President himself had appointed. Kennedy's hope had been that the committee would win conservatives to foreign aid, but the plan went askew. In the opinion of John Sherman Cooper, foreign aid benefited little under Kennedy, aside from some additional funds for Latin America. In Africa Kennedy did not seek out the kinds of rightist regimes that over the years have so beguiled us in Latin America. Washington showed no sympathy for the white supremacist government of South Africa and strongly supported the efforts of the United Nations to put down a secessionist movement in Katanga considered to be more friendly to Western neoimperialism than was the new government of the Congo.

Chapter 18 RECKLESS AND RUTHLESS

PETER COLLIER (b. 1939) and DAVID HOROWITZ (b. 1939) are California writers who have collaborated since the early 1960s on articles and books. In their pathbreaking *The Kennedys: An American Drama* they frankly discuss Cuba, Judith Campbell Exner, and Operation Mongoose, tying Jack and Bobby Kennedy directly to reckless and immoral activity. How much attention should be paid to the Kennedy "machismo"?

. . . while Jack became more elusive in office, disappearing into the mythic status of the presidency, Bobby was just the opposite, becoming daily more real. Jack's face had changed dramatically over the years, filling out even to the point of jowliness, partly as a result of the steroids he took. He would finger his cheek while looking in the mirror and say, "That's not my face." Bobby's face hadn't changed much over the years except perhaps to become more distinctively his own. The eyes were capable, as one woman said, of boring through someone; his nose like a raptor's beak, his jaw set aggressively: he was the Kennedy soldier, perpetually on duty.

"Bobby stories," little epiphanies of ruthlessness, were common fare on the Washington cocktail circuit. How, at a Hickory Hill dinner, he asked Averell Harriman if he had seen a directive he had issued restricting the travel of Eastern European diplomats, and when Harriman said he had seen it and was planning to get to it soon, Bobby had slammed his hand down on the table and told the august diplomat in tones appropriate to reprimand a twenty-five-year-old foreign service officer: "You get on that first thing in the morning!" How he had begun legal proceedings against his father's companion in philandering, Igor Cassini, for not registering as an agent for the Dominican Republic, and against Jim Landis, his father's one-time aide who had written speeches for Jack and had been a family loyalist for years but had neglected to file income tax returns. "Little Brother Is Watching You" became a sort of password among people who ran afoul of the Attorney General.

But Bobby didn't care what was said about him. He had taken upon himself responsibility for the success or failure of the New Frontier. And by the spring of 1962, he seemed to be trying to cover the whole of its vast geography. In addition to ongoing crises such as civil rights, there were daily problems such as the steel crisis, during which he sent FBI agents out in the middle of the night to subpoena the steel company executives who seemed to be defying his brother on the issue of price rises. And there was still his unofficial but increasingly obsessive role as general of the secret war against Castro.

Roswell Gilpatric, another member of the Special Group (Augmented) later said that Bobby was the "moving spirit" behind Operation Mongoose. Time and again he would come to meetings complaining that plans were inadequate: "We should get in there and do more." He put in calls to Richard Helms, who had replaced the hapless [Richard] Bissell, to check progress on the planned acts of sabotage and subversion. ("My God, these Kennedys keep the pressure on about Castro," the taciturn Helms finally complained to CIA attorney Lawrence Houston.) One of [General Edward] Lansdale's plans which particularly seized Bobby's imagination called for sabotage of the Matahambre copper mines. He was on the phone constantly about it: "Had the agents landed? Had they reached the mines? Had they destroyed them?"

In Lansdale's original plan, Mongoose was to have been a modest program one of whose benefits would be to keep the CIA's appetite for power in check. But by the spring Mongoose was growing apace. Soon the Miami headquarters of Task Force W, the Agency's arm for implementing plans conceived by the Special Group (Augmented), was on its way to becoming the largest CIA installation in the world, one that would ultimately involve five hundred case workers handling some three thousand Cubans at an expense of more than $100 million per year. Bobby was often there to spur them on. More than once he came into conflict with William Harvey, the corpulent, paranoid CIA operative in charge of Task Force W who had become something of a legend in the Agency. (One of these confrontations took place in the Miami headquarters during one of Bobby's visits. After reading the classified messages on the teletype, he tore a strip off and was taking it with him to the door when Harvey yelled: "Hey, where are you going with that?" When Bobby kept on walking, Harvey rushed over to block his way and grabbed the message out of his hand.)

But claustral though it came to seem to those involved in planning, the clandestine assaults on Cuba did not take place in a vacuum. Early in 1962, Jack set up a Special Group for counterinsurgency which was supposed to confront the problem of guerrillas in Southeast Asia and other regions where the U.S. had interests that were challenged, and prevent them from coming to power as they had with Castro. Again [General Maxwell] Taylor was in charge; again Bobby was the most enthusiastic member.

Some members of the administration felt that the talk about counterinsurgency always remained an intellectual dalliance for Jack. With Bobby it had clearly become a sort of mania, an elaboration on a global scale of his earlier "chasing bad men." He kept a green beret on his desk. He imported Special Forces troops for weekend exercises at Hyannis, efforts which Sargent Shriver, far less enthusiastic about the clandestine world of derring-do, referred to as "swinging from trees and hanging from fences" and refused to let his children watch.

Early in 1962, Bobby, in Saigon on a stopover during a Far Eastern trip, said: "This is a new kind of war, but war it is in a very real sense of the word. It is a war fought not by massive divisions but secretly by terror, assassination, ambush and infiltration. . . . I think the United States will do what is necessary to help a country that is trying to repel aggression with its own blood, tears and sweat. . . .

The way Bobby moved between committees and agencies—partly as Jack's ombudsman to make sure there were no more disasters, but also as a goad making sure that the darker purposes of the administration were accomplished—was wholly extraordinary. The blood tie was crucial to this unique role. Only the President's brother could have dogged the intelligence bureaucracy the way he did; only a brother could have overridden the checks and balances present even in the secret reaches of government to accomplish the ends he and Jack had in mind. But if brotherhood was his great advantage, it was also the cross Bobby bore, for the more deeply he involved himself in Jack's behalf the more he saw how flawed his brother was. The fullest realization came on February 27, 1962, when he received a memo from J. Edgar Hoover stating that information developed in connection with an FBI investigation showed that Judith Campbell, one of Jack's mistresses since 1960, was also the mistress of Chicago Mafia capo Sam Giancana. . . .

The revelation of the Giancana-Campbell part of the triangle was more than a moral disaster; it was a political one as well. It was bad enough to be under [J. Edgar] Hoover's thumb once again. (Bobby later said that the FBI Director had been sending a memo every month or so "about someone I knew or a member of my family or allegations in connection with myself so that it would be clear . . . . he was on top of all these things . . . .") But even worse, the people he hated most—the chieftains of organized crime—now had a hold on his brother and on the presidency itself.

There was, moreover, an obvious thread leading from the relationship with Campbell to the potentially devastating subject of murder plots against Castro in the works since August 1960, about the same time Bissell was beginning to plan the Bay of Pigs and running on a parallel line. Some of these plots seemed almost to have been designed by a gag writer: using depilatories to make the Cuban leader lose his beard and therefore his machismo; killing him by contaminating one of his favorite cigars with botulism. But there was a more serious dimension and it centered on the CIA's decision to use the mob, another party aggrieved by the Castro revolution, to stage a hit. As its middleman for the plot, the CIA had recruited Robert Maheu, a former FBI agent working for Howard Hughes. Maheu brought in Las Vegas hoodlum John Roselli, who in turn brought in Giancana, an associate of former Havana Cosa Nostra boss Santos Trafficante. Not long before the Bay of Pigs, an attempt was made to slip poison pills into Castro's food; afterward efforts were suspended. The whole matter of mob involvement in assassination plots had come up only because Giancana asked Maheu as a favor to bug the Las Vegas hotel room of comedian Dan Rowan, who he suspected was sleeping with another Giancana girlfriend, singer Phyllis McGuire, and the FBI discovered the bug.

In May, Bobby was briefed about the whole situation. CIA men Lawrence Houston and Colonel Sheffield Edwards later recalled that he heatedly responded that if the Agency was going to become involved with gangsters again, he wanted to be informed first, although he did not comment on the operation itself. If Bobby gave the impression of anger rather than surprise—"If you have seen [his] eyes get steely and his jaw set and his voice get low and precise," Houston said, "you get a definite feeling of unhappiness"—it was because he already knew that Giancana had been used by the CIA against Castro, having been informed by Hoover a year earlier, in a memo dated May 22, 1961. And on April 8, scarcely a month before his briefing, another CIA contact had been made with Johnny Roselli at which the mobster was given more poison pills to use on Castro. According to William Harvey, Colonel Edwards had made the April contact with Roselli.

In the tangled dramaturgy of events, it was not clear who had been directly responsible for the assassination plans. No one ever specified that Jack or Bobby had officially ordered them. Yet Richard Helms later noted that no official order would have been required. An intimation would have been enough, as when Henry I asked his antagonist Beckett: Will nobody rid me of this troublesome priest?

In any case, assassination was certainly in the air. In January 1961, Bissell had created "Executive Action," telling Harvey—in words he would later confirm in official testimony but disclaim after a talk with [Walt] Rostow and [McGeorge] Bundy—that the White House had twice urged him to build such an assassination capacity. As early as November 1961, the President had brought *New York Times* Latin American expert Tad Szulc into the Oval Office, allegedly to look him over for a job in the administration but actually to hold a peculiar conversation. "What would you think if I ordered Castro to be assassinated?" the President asked out of the blue. Szulc said he was against it and Jack said he was too. "He said he was testing me, that he felt the same way . . ." Szulc said later, "because indeed the U.S. morally must not be a party to assassinations." Szulc always wondered if this conversation had anything to do with the fact that he had caught wind of an abortive scheme by which U.S. military intelligence would have infiltrated a band of Cuban exile marksmen into Cuba from the U.S. base at Guantanamo to stage a hit on Fidel and his brother Raúl.

As late as August 10, 1962, when the Special Group (Augmented) met in Rusk's office to discuss Mongoose, McNamara brought up anew the question of killing Castro, and Ed Murrow, then head of the United States Information Agency, and others took sharp exception. "It was the obvious consensus. . . ," the irascible Harvey wrote in a memo about the meeting, "in answer to a comment by Mr. Ed Murrow, that this is not a subject which has been made a matter of official record." Three days later, Lansdale drafted a new plan of operation for Mongoose and asked Harvey to prepare papers on several subjects: "Intelligence, Political (including liquidation of leaders), Economic (sabotage, limited deception), and Paramilitary." Harvey exploded at the indiscretion, calling Lansdale to point out "the inadmissibility and stupidity of putting this type of comment in writing in such a document" and asserting that the CIA would "write no document pertaining to this and would participate in no open meeting discussing it."

The fact that the Giancana-Campbell-JFK triangle threatened to make such plots public now made it all the more vital that Bobby do something. Since he could not really prosecute Giancana, he ordered around-the-clock harassment of him. FBI men parked outside the mobster's house; they followed him so closely on the golf course that he later claimed he lost twenty strokes off his game. When he finally petitioned a court for relief, the Justice Department ordered the federal attorney assigned to the case to decline to cross-examine him. It was also at this time that Bobby cut ties with Giancana's friend and business partner, Frank Sinatra. ("Johnny, you just can't associate with this guy," Red Fay recalls hearing him say to Jack.)

Chapter 19 THE MISSILE CRISIS

I. F. STONE (1907-89) was a highly-regarded left-wing journalist. From 1953 to 1971 he published *I. F. Stone's Weekly*. From 1975 until his death, he was a scholar in residence at American University. In this excerpt, a column from 1966, Stone examines the dangers involved in the Cuban missile crisis. How much credit should Khurshchev be given for ending a confrontation he initiated?

The essential, the terrifying, question about the missile crisis is what would have happened if Khrushchev had not backed down. It is extraordinary, in the welter of magazine articles and books dealing with the missile crisis, how rarely this question is raised. The story is told and retold as a test and triumph of the Kennedy brothers. But the deeper reaches of the story are avoided, as if we feared to look too closely into the larger implications of this successful first foray into nuclear brinkmanship. We may not be so lucky next time.

The public impression created by the government when the presence of the missiles in Cuba was verified is that they represented a direct threat to America's cities. For those a little more sophisticated it was said that they threatened the balance of power. Elie Abel's book on *The Missile Crisis*, like the earlier accounts by Sorensen and

From *In A Time Of Torment* by I. F. Stone, copyright 1968. Reprinted by permission of Random House, Inc. and Jonathan Cape Ltd.

Schlesinger, shows that this was not the dominant view in the inner councils of the White House. Abel quotes McNamara as saying, "A missile is a missile. It makes no great difference whether you are killed by a missile fired from the Soviet Union or from Cuba." But in the week of argument, Abel relates, McNamara came to concede that even if the effect on the strategic balance was relatively small, "the political effect in Latin America and elsewhere would be large." As Sorensen wrote in his *Kennedy*, "To be sure, these Cuban missiles alone, in view of all the other megatonnage the Soviets were capable of unleashing upon us, did not substantially alter the strategic balance *in fact* . . . But that balance would have been substantially altered *in appearance* (italics in original); and in matters of national will and world leadership, as the President said later, such appearances contribute to reality." The real stake was prestige.

The question was whether, with the whole world looking on, Kennedy would let Khrushchev get away with it. The world's first thermonuclear confrontation turned out to be a kind of ordeal by combat between two men to see which one would back down first. Schlesinger relates that in the earlier Berlin crisis, he wrote a memorandum to Kennedy protesting the tendency to define the issue as "Are you chicken or not?" But inescapably that's what the issue came around to. Schlesinger recounts an interview Kennedy gave James Wechsler of the *New York Post* in the Berlin crisis in which the President recognized that no one could win a nuclear war, that "the only alternatives were authentic negotiation or mutual annihilation," *but—*

> What worried him (Kennedy) was that Khrushchev might interpret his reluctance to wage nuclear war as a symptom of an American loss of nerve . . . ." If Khrushchev wants to rub my nose in the dirt," he told Wechsler, "it's all over."

At a Book and Author lunch Abel recounted a story which should have been in his book. He told of a visit to the President in September, 1961, after the Bay of Pigs and the Berlin wall. Abel told Kennedy he wanted to write a book about the Administration's first year. "Who," the President asked despondently, "would want to read a book about disasters?" He felt that Khrushchev, after these two debacles, might think him a pushover. James Reston of the *New York Times*, who saw Kennedy emerge "shaken and angry" from his meeting with Khrushchev in Vienna, speculates that Khrushchev had studied the Bay of Pigs. "He would have understood if Kennedy had left Castro alone or destroyed him; but when Kennedy was rash enough to strike at Cuba but not bold enough to finish the job, Khrushchev decided he was dealing with an inexperienced young leader who could be intimidated and blackmailed." There was an intensely personal note in the Kennedy broadcast which announced the quarantine of Cuba. "This secret, swift and extraordinary buildup of communist missiles . . . . is a deliberately provocative and unjustified change in the status quo which cannot be accepted by this country, if *our courage* (my italics) and our commitments are ever to be trusted again by either friend or foe." It was the courage of John F. Kennedy which was in question, the credibility of his readiness to go the whole way if the missiles were not removed. In the eyeball to eyeball confrontation, it was Khrushchev who was forced to blink first.

This was magnificent as drama. It was the best of therapies for Kennedy's nagging inferiority complex. Like any other showdown between the leaders of two contending hordes or tribes, it was also not without wider political significance. Certainly the fright it gave Khrushchev and the new sense of confidence it gave Kennedy were factors in the *detente* which followed. The look into the abyss made both men really feel in their bones the need for co-existence. But one may wonder how many Americans, consulted in a swift electronic plebiscite, would have cared to risk destruction to let John F. Kennedy prove himself.

A curious aspect of all three accounts, Sorensen's, Schlesinger's, and Abel's, is how they slide over Kennedy's immediate political situation. There might have been dispute as to whether those missiles in Cuba really represented any change in the balance of terror, any substantial new threat to the United States. There could have been no dispute that to face the November elections with these missiles intact would have been disastrous for Kennedy and the Democrats. The first alarms about missiles in Cuba, whether justified or not at the time, had been raised by the Republican Senator Keating. President Kennedy had assured the country on September 4 that the only missiles in Cuba were anti-aircraft with a twenty-five-mile range and on September 13 that new Soviet shipments to Cuba were not a "serious threat." The election was only three weeks off when the presence of nuclear missiles on the island was confirmed on October 15 by aerial photographs. There was no time for prolonged negotiations, summit conferences, or UN debates if the damage was to be undone before the election. Kennedy could not afford to wait. This gamble paid off when he was able on October 28 to "welcome" Khrushchev's "statesmanlike decision" to dismantle the missiles, and on November 2, four days before the election, to announce that they were being crated for removal. But what if the gamble had failed? What if Khrushchev, instead of backing down when he did, had engaged in a delaying action, offering to abide by the outcome of a United Nations debate? The Republicans would have accused Kennedy of gullibility and weakness; the nuclear menace from Cuba would certainly have cost the Democrats control of the House of Representatives. After the Bays of Pigs fiasco, the damage to Kennedy's reputation might have been irreparable even if ultimately some peaceful deal to get the missiles out of Cuba were achieved. Kennedy could not wait. But the country and the world could. Negotiations, however prolonged, would have been better than the risk of World War III. This is how the survivors would have felt. Here Kennedy's political interests and the country's safety diverged.

Could these political considerations have been as absent from the discussions and the minds of the Kennedy inner circle as the accounts of the two in-house historians, Sorensen and Schlesinger, and that of Abel would lead us to believe? Sorensen touches on the subject ever so tactfully at only one point. He relates that during the White

House debates on what to do about the missiles, a Republican participant passed him a note saying:

> Ted—have you considered the very real possibility that if we allow Cuba to complete installation and operational readiness of missile bases, the next House of Representatives is likely to have a Republican majority? This would completely paralyze our ability to react sensibly and coherently to further Soviet advances.

Given the choice between the danger of a Republican majority in the House and the danger of a thermonuclear war, voters might conceivably have thought the former somewhat less frightening and irreversible.

Sorensen paints a sentimental, touching picture of Kennedy on the eve of the confrontation. "He spoke on the back porch on that Saturday before his speech not of his possible death but of all the innocent children of the world who had never had a chance or a voice." If Kennedy was so concerned he might have sacrificed his chances in the election to try and negotiate. It is difficult to reconcile this concern with the "consternation" Schlesinger reports when Radio Moscow broadcast a Khrushchev letter offering removal of its missiles from Cuba and a non-aggression pledge to Turkey if the U.S. would remove its missiles from Turkey and offer a non-aggression pledge to Cuba. This had been widely suggested at home and abroad, by Lippmann and many others, as a mutual face-saver. "But Kennedy," Schlesinger writes, "regarded the idea as unacceptable, and the swap was promptly rejected."

Abel recalls that early in 1961 the Joint Congressional Committee on Atomic Energy had recommended removal of these missiles from both Italy and Turkey as "unreliable, inaccurate, obsolete, and too easily sabotaged." He reveals that Kennedy in the late summer of 1961 gave orders for their removal. "It was therefore with a double sense of shock," Abel writes, "that Kennedy heard the news that Saturday morning. Not only were the missiles still in Turkey but they had just become pawns in a deadly chess game." Would it have been so unthinkable a sacrifice to have swapped those obsolete missiles, which Kennedy removed so soon afterward anyway?

Abel's account indicates that the Kennedy brothers were unwilling to be put in the position of paying any but the most minimal price for peace. Khrushchev's surrender had to be all but unconditional. Abel tells us that Adlai Stevenson at the White House conference on October 20 "forecast grave difficulties" at the UN "concerning the Jupiter bases in Turkey. People would certainly ask why it was right for the United States to have bases in Turkey but wrong for the Russians to have bases in Cuba." He also urged the President to consider offering to withdraw from Guantanamo as part of a plan to demilitarize, neutralize, and guarantee the territorial integrity of Cuba. Both ideas were rejected. "The bitter aftertaste of that Saturday afternoon in the Oval Room," Abel writes, "stayed with him (Stevenson) until his death. It was after this encounter that Robert Kennedy decided Stevenson lacked the toughness to deal effectively with the Russians at the UN" and suggested to the President "that John

McCloy or Herman Phleger, the California Republican who had served as chief legal advisor to John Foster Dulles, be asked to help in the UN negotiations. McCloy got the job."

All these accounts are appallingly ethnocentric. Cuba's fate and interests are simply ignored. Neither Abel nor Schlesinger nor Sorensen mentions that two weeks earlier President Dorticos of Cuba in a speech to the General Assembly on October 8—before the presence of the missiles in Cuba had been verified—said his country was ready for demilitarization if the U.S. gave assurances "by word and by deed, that it would not commit acts of aggression against our country." This speech contained a cryptic reference to "our unavoidable weapons—weapons that we wish we did not need and that we do not want to use." This was ignored by the American press. Though Stevenson, we now learn from Abel, was soon to favor demilitarization of Cuba, his public reply on October 8 was the State Department line, "The maintenance of communism in the Americans is not negotiable."

All these possibilities for negotiating a way out indicate that the Cuban missile crisis was not one of those thermonuclear crises requiring instant response and leaving no time for negotiation and no time for consultation. The situation fits that described by George Kennan when he came back from Belgrade in August 1961 and said, "There is no presumption more terrifying than that of those who would blow up the world on the basis of their personal judgment of a transient situation. I do not propose to let the future of the world be settled, or ended, by a group of men operating on the basis of limited perspectives and short-run calculations." Schlesinger quotes Kennan's words to show the atmosphere of those "strange, moody days." He does not, of course, apply them to the missile crisis. Kennan's anguish may seem that of an outsider, without access to what the insiders alone know. But Sorensen says that at one time in the inner debate Kennedy and his circle "seriously considered" either doing nothing about the missiles or limiting our response to diplomatic action only. "As some (but not all) Pentagon advisors pointed out to the President," Sorensen reveals, "we had long lived within range of Soviet missiles, we expected Khrushchev to live with our missiles nearby, and by taking this addition calmly we would prevent him from inflating its importance."

There was fear in the inner circle that our Western allies might share this cool estimate. Perhaps this was one reason we did not consult them before deciding on a showdown. As Sorensen writes, "Most West Europeans cared nothing about Cuba and thought we were over-anxious about it. Would they support our risking a world war, or an attack on NATO member Turkey, or a move on West Berlin, because we now had a few dozen hostile missiles nearby?" Similarly Schlesinger reveals that Macmillan, when informed of Kennedy's plans, was troubled "because Europeans had grown so accustomed to living under the nuclear gun that they might wonder what all the fuss was about."

To consult was to invite advice we did not wish to hear. Abel reveals that when Acheson arrived as the President's special emissary to let De Gaulle know what was afoot, "De Gaulle raised his hand in a delaying gesture that the long departed kings of France might have envied," and asked, "Are you consulting or informing me?" When Acheson confessed that he was there to inform not consult, De Gaulle said dryly, "I am in favor of international decisions." But three years later De Gaulle was to make an independent decision of his own and ask NATO to remove its bases in France. One reason for this was the Cuban missile crisis. As De Gaulle said at his last press conference February 21:

> . . . while the prospects of a world war breaking out on account of Europe are dissipating conflicts in which America engages in other parts of the world—as the day before yesterday in Korea, yesterday in Cuba, today in Vietnam—risk, by virtue of that famous escalation, being extended so that the result would be a general conflagration. In that case Europe—whose strategy is, within NATO, that of America—would be automatically involved in the struggle, even when it would not have so desired . . . France's determination to dispose of herself . . . is incompatible with a defense organization in which she finds herself subordinate.

Had the Cuban missile crisis erupted into a thermonuclear exchange, NATO bases in France would automatically have been involved: They would have joined in the attack and been targets for the Russians. France, like the other NATO countries, might have been destroyed without ever being consulted. It is not difficult to understand De Gaulle's distrust of an alliance in which the strongest member can plunge all the others into war without consulting them.

Kennedy no more consulted NATO before deciding to risk world war over Cuba than Khrushchev consulted his Warsaw Pact satellites before taking the risky step of placing missiles on the island. The objection to Khrushchev's course, as to Kennedy's, was primarily political rather than military. There is general agreement now that the Russians may have been tempted to put missiles in Cuba to redress in some small part the enormous missile gap against them which McNamara disclosed after Kennedy took office; for this view we can cite, among other studies, a Rand Corporation memorandum written for the Air Force by Arnold L. Horelick. In retrospect the Air Force turned out to be the victim of its own ingenuity in developing the U-2. So long as the U.S. had to depend on surmise and normal intelligence, it was possible to inflate the estimates of Russian missile strength to support the demand for larger Air Force appropriations; hence first a bomber gap and then a missile gap, both of which turned out to be nonexistent. But when the U-2s began to bring back precise information, the nightmarish missile computations hawked by such Air Force mouthpieces as Stuart Symington and Joseph Alsop began to be deflated. Despite the sober warnings of Eisenhower and Allen Dulles that there was no missile gap, the Democrats used it in the 1960 campaign only to find on taking office that the gap was the other way. Militarily the missiles on Cuba didn't make too much difference. Even the Horelick study for the Air Force admits that these missiles "would presumably have been highly vulnerable to a U.S. first strike, even with conventional bombs," and their number was too small for a Soviet first strike. "Moreover," Horelick writes, "there would have been a problem, though perhaps not an insurmountable one, of coordinating salvoes from close-in and distant bases so as to avoid a ragged attack." (If missiles were fired at the same time from Cuba and Russia, the ones from nearby Cuba would have landed so far in advance as to give additional warning time.) Their deployment in Cuba bears all the earmarks of one of those febrile improvisations to which the impulsive Khrushchev was given, as in his proposals for a "troika" control of the United Nations.

Khrushchev was guilty of a foolish duplicity. Gromyko gave Kennedy a message from Khrushchev that he would suspend any action about Berlin until after the November election so as not to embarrass Kennedy. This and a Tass communique of September 11 made Kennedy and his advisers feel certain that the Russians would not upset the situation by secretly placing nuclear missiles in Cuba. Tass said the Soviet Union's nuclear weapons were so powerful and its rockets so wide-ranging "that there is no need to search for sites for them beyond the boundaries of the Soviet Union." How could Khrushchev hope to negotiate with Kennedy when the President discovered that he had been so grossly gulled? By first installing the missiles and then telling an easily detected lie about so serious a matter, Khrushchev shares responsibility with Kennedy for bringing the world to its first thermonuclear brink.

Because Kennedy succeeded and Khrushchev surrendered, the missile crisis is being held up as a model of how to run a confrontation in the thermonuclear age. In his February 17, 1966, statement advocating negotiations with the Vietcong, and offering them a place in a future government, Senator Robert F. Kennedy said Hanoi "must be given to understand as well that their present public demands are in fact for us to surrender a vital national interest—but that, as a far larger and more powerful nation learned in October of 1962, surrender of a vital interest of the United States is an objective which cannot be achieved." In the missile crisis the Kennedys played their dangerous game skillfully. They kept their means and aims sharply limited, resisting pressures to bomb the island and to demand the removal of Castro as well as the missiles. For this restraint we are indebted to the Kennedys. But all their skill would have been to no avail if in the end Khrushchev had preferred his prestige, as they preferred theirs, to the danger of a world war. In this respect we are all indebted to Khrushchev.

The missile crisis is a model of what to avoid. This is the lesson John F. Kennedy learned. "His feelings," Schlesinger writes in the finest passage of his *A Thousand Days*, "underwent a qualitative change after Cuba: A world in which nations threatened each other with nuclear weapons now seemed to him not just an irrational but an intolerable and impossible world. Cuba thus made vivid the sense that all humanity had a common interest in the prevention of nuclear war—an interest far above those national and ideological interests which had once seemed ultimate." This, and not the saga of a lucky hairbreadth balancing act on an abyss, is what most needs to be remembered about the missile crisis, if we are to avoid another.

Chapter 20 VIETNAM

The best scholarly study to date of the Kennedy Administration is by HERBERT S. PARMET (q.v.). Here, from *JFK, The Presidency Of John F. Kennedy*, the historian discusses Administration policy toward Southeast Asia. How strong is the evidence that JFK was prepared to go all-out to defend South Vietnam from the Communists?

When Ambassador Frederick Nolting's tour of duty expired that summer, the President replaced him by sending Henry Cabot Lodge, Jr., to Saigon. . . .

The most intriguing possibility eventually raised is that Lodge was sent to effectuate the overthrow of Diem by working with the generals who hoped to bring about a coup. Lodge has explained that Kennedy was very much disturbed by the picture of the monk on fire. He talked about the overall reportage of what was going on in Saigon and said that the Diem government was entering a terminal phase. The American embassy had also had poor press relations. "I suppose that there are worse press relations to be found in the world today," Lodge remembered that the President told him, "and I wish you would take charge of press relations." As far as helping to overthrow Diem, Kennedy said that the "Vietnamese are doing that for themselves and don't need any outside help."

Almost immediately after that, Diem helped to speed his own downfall. Just before Lodge's arrival, in complete contradiction of a promise made to Ambassador Nolting, Nhu's American-trained Special Forces went on a rampage against Buddhist pagodas in Hué, Saigon, and other cities. More than fourteen hundred Buddhists were arrested. Right after that American intelligence also reported that Diem was actively engaged in trying to work out a deal with the Hanoi regime of North Vietnam.

If Lodge had been sent with an understanding that he might have to support the generals wanting to get rid of Diem, his actions appeared to confirm that purpose. He showed as little outward support toward the South Vietnamese president as possible, disassociating himself almost completely. On August 24, with Kennedy at Hyannis Port and, "by a strange coincidence, most of the other senior members of the administration" out of town for the weekend, word arrived that South Vietnamese generals knew that Ngo Dinh Nhu was negotiating with the Communists. The information was relayed to Washington via long-distance telephone by Admiral Harry Felt.

Quickly on that Saturday, after a series of consultations and telephone calls— including to the President, Forrestal, and Hilsman—Harriman sent a cable to Lodge in the name of the State Department. Its message was clear: The U.S. could no longer tolerate a situation where power remained in Nhu's hands. "We wish to give Diem reasonable opportunity to remove Nhus, but if he remains obdurate, then we are prepared to accept the obvious implications that we can no longer support Diem. You may also tell appropriate military commanders we will give them direct support in any interim period of breakdown central goverment mechanism." Lodge cabled back that it was most unlikely that Diem would get rid of both his brother and sister-in-law and that Nhu was in control of the combat forces in Saigon. "Therefore," he replied, "propose we go straight to Generals with our demands, without informing Diem. Would tell them we prepared to have Diem without Nhus but it is in effect up to them whether to keep him.

For a time it almost seemed that it was the American State Department, in the absence of Dean Rusk, Robert McNamara, John McCone, or McGeorge Bundy, that had undertaken its own coup against those who continued to believe that there was little choice but to back Diem. General Maxwell Taylor first heard about the cable when Ros Gilpatric called him that evening at Fort Myer with the information that clearance from the President had already been obtained and that, in Rusk's absence, George Ball had consented while playing golf. Gilpatric has since observed that "I frankly thought it was an end run. I didn't see why it had to be done Saturday night with the President away, with Rusk away, with McNamara away, Bundy away. I was suspicious of the circumstances in which it was being done. . . . In other words the Defense and military were brought in sort of after the fact." To General Taylor it seemed somewhat of a *fait accompli*. Even if Diem wanted to comply, the telegram to

Lodge was obviously an open encouragement "to plotters to move against him at any time."

Mike Forrestal agrees that the circumstances indeed were suspicious. Harriman had originated the cable. The senior diplomat, by then under-secretary of state for political affairs, wanted to take advantage of the weekend conditions because he knew how much trouble he would have getting support if everybody were present. Still, the most important—and often the least noticed element—was the endorsement that came from the President himself, not at the center of action in the Oval Office, but at the other end of a wire in Hyannis Port.

But there was no immediate result. The cable had advised the Voice of America radio people to publicize only that part of the message that would prevent the Vietnamese army from being associated with any plot. Hilsman tried to work that out by briefing a news correspondent so the information could be fed to the Voice, thereby maintaining the usual procedure according to which the propaganda network operated. But the people who actually made the broadcast failed to check their instructions with a telegram sent to guide them. The entire story then went out on the airwaves, "not only," as Hilsman wrote, "that the United States had proof that the Vietnamese Army was innocent of the assault on the pagodas and that Nhu's secret police and Special Forces were to blame," but about the threatened sharp American reduction of aid to Diem.

At a meeting in the embassy in Saigon, Lodge was furious. "Jack Kennedy would never approve of doing things this way," he shouted. "This certainly isn't his way of running a government."

When the President returned from the Cape and met with his staff that Monday, he found more opposition to the Harriman cable than he had evidently expected. "And so the government split in two," the attorney general later said. "It was the only time really, in three years, the government was broken in two in a very disturbing way." In Saigon the generals were unable to get the backing of key army units and remained uncertain, despite CIA assurances, of what American intelligence would do, and withheld any actions.

When the coup came, it resulted from the appropriate opening, which was a combination of the muffled hand from Washington and changed circumstances in Saigon. In the interim Kennedy's customary indecision made the entire process seem more diabolical than it was. First of all the failed move of August provided an opportunity to reassess the situation. At the end of the month Lodge cabled that there was "no turning back" from the overthrow. American prestige was already too committed. Kennedy sent him a personal and private message that pledged his full support to enable his ambassador to "conclude this operation successfully," and, with the clear memory of what happened at the Bay of Pigs, added, "I know from experience that failure is more destructive than an appearance of indecision." On September 2, after De Gaulle had criticized the American involvement in Vietnam, Kennedy was interviewed by Walter Cronkite on a CBS television news program. At that point, in response to a question about Diem changing his pattern, the President answered in a manner that has too often been quoted incompletely. What he said at that point was: "We hope that he comes to see that, but in the final analysis it is the people and the government itself who have to win or lose this struggle. All we can do is help, and we are making it very clear, but I don't agree with those who say we should withdraw. That would be a great mistake." It was not immediately evident that, in reality, he was talking just as much about the Vietnamese choice of a leader as about the American commitment. On the same day that he talked to Cronkite, Kennedy called Hilsman and asked whether his undersecretary of state had done any thinking about "selective cuts in aid that would not hurt the war effort but still make Diem and Nhu understand that we mean business." Encouragement was also given to Senator Church's threat to introduce a resolution calling for the suspension of aid to South Vietnam unless it ended its repressive policies. During this period, however, the President had no way of knowing that things in Saigon would be better without Diem. But his hand was being pushed. An Alsop story in *The Washington Post* on September 18, evidently based on interviews with Diem and Nhu, gave further information about their dealings with Hanoi. Reacting to such stories, Kennedy sent McNamara and General Taylor to Saigon. Once again Diem was immovable, contending that the war was going well, pointing with pride to favorable results from just completed rigged elections, and, as McNamara wrote, offering "absolutely no assurances that he would take any steps in response to the representations made to American visitors. . . . His manner was one of at least outward serenity and of a man who had patiently explained a great deal and who hoped he had thus corrected a number of misapprehensions." The McNamara-Taylor report, however, cautioned that it was not the time to take the initiative in trying to change the government. "Our policy should be to seek urgently to identify and build contacts with an alternative leadership if and when it appears." Mainly the suggestion of the mission was to apply selective pressures on the regime.

On October 2 the White House announced that a thousand men would be withdrawn by the end of the year. Gilpatric later stated that McNamara did indicate to him that the withdrawal was part of the President's plan to wind down the war, but, that was too far in the future. They were still, at that moment, deeply divided about what to do about the internal situation in Saigon. At just that point the recall of John Richardson, the CIA station chief who was close to the regime, seemed to be another signal, although it may not have been intended for that purpose. Still, it is hard to believe that the move, along with the talk about reductions of American aid to the government, lacked the purpose of giving further encouragement to the anti-Diem generals.

During a series of meetings that were held from August 23 through October 23 between Lodge, General Harkins, and the anti-Diem plotters, including Duong Van Minh (Big Minh), there was agreement on what had to be done: The U.S. agreed that Nhu had to go and that the disposition of Diem ought to be left to the generals. There could be no American help to initiate the action, but support would come during the interim period in case of a breakdown of the central government's mechanism. What was also clear was that if they did not get rid of the Nhus and the Buddhist situation were not redressed, the United States would end economic and military support.

Lodge later reported that he had advised the President "not to thwart" a coup. That act, rather than initiating one, would have constituted interference. Yet even at that point Kennedy wavered, suffering a recurrence of earlier doubts. He told Bundy that the U.S. should be in a position to blow the whistle if it looked as though the coup was failing. Bundy cabled Lodge that there should be no American action that would reveal any knowledge that a coup was even possible. The "burden of proof" must be on the plotters "to show a substantial possibility of quick success; otherwise we should discourage them from proceeding since a miscalculation could result in jeopardizing U.S. position in Southeast Asia." Indeed, the Americans in Saigon behaved as though things were normal.

On the morning of November 1 Admiral Felt paid a courtesy call on Diem at the presidential palace. In the afternoon Diem called Lodge to ask about the American attitude toward the coup. Lodge was evasive, but admitted he was worried about Diem's personal safety. That night, the president and Nhu escaped from the palace to a hideout in the Chinese quarter of Saigon. From there Diem contacted the generals and asked for safe conduct back so he could make a graceful exit from power. On his return, however, according to a prearranged plan, he and his brother were shot and killed by Big Minh's personal bodyguard.

The news of Diem's death outraged Kennedy. General Taylor wrote that he "leaped to his feet and rushed from the room with a look of shock and dismay on his feet and rushed from the room with a look of shock and dismay on his face which I had never seen before." George Smathers remembered that Jack Kennedy blamed the CIA, saying "I've got to do something about those bastards"; they should be stripped of their exorbitant power. Mike Forrestal called Kennedy's reaction "both personal and religious," and especially troubled by the implication that a Catholic President had participated in a plot to assassinate a coreligionist. Every account of Kennedy's response is in complete agreement. Until the very end he had hoped Diem's life could be spared.

It has now become clear that however futile his efforts Kennedy tried to prevent the murder. He told Francis Cardinal Spellman that he had known in advance that the Vietnamese leader would probably be killed, but in the end he could not control the situation. At least one attempt, and possibly three, came from a direct attempt to communicate with Diem by using a personal emissary, someone completely loyal to Jack Kennedy, someone totally without any other obligation, his intimate friend, Torby Macdonald, the Massachusetts congressman.

As far as is known, there are no written records. It was completely secret. Mike Forrestal remembers briefing Macdonald for the trip. Torbert Macdonald, Jr., recalls that his father told him about it. The congressman's widow is certain that he made at least three trips to Saigon for the President. Torby's closest friend during his final years, who desires to remain anonymous, has a photograph of him posing before the ancient temple at Angkor-Wat in Cambodia, indicating that he went through that country while traveling to South Vietnam as a private citizen.

Macdonald himself explained why Kennedy sent him. The President had begun to develop personal sources of information from FBI men who were bypassing J. Edgar Hoover and going directly to him. Some CIA people were following a similar route and avoiding the Agency. By that time the President was learning. When he first came into office, he had been intimidated by the Pentagon and the CIA, but he had begun to find out how to get around them. When he heard that Big Minh and his group were planning to assassinate Diem, he wanted to make a direct contact. He was hesitant about using the embassy in Saigon because he could not trust his own people there. Nor did he have enough confidence in Lodge, who had maintained a distant relationship with Diem. Finally, there was no South Vietnamese he could trust. So he called on Torby, who then carried the President's personal plea, which was to get rid of his brother and take refuge in the American embassy. As Macdonald later explained it, he told Diem: "They're going to kill you. You've got to get out of there temporarily to seek sanctuary in the American embassy and you must rid of your sister-in-law and your brother." But Diem refused. "He just won't do it," Macdonald reported to the president. "He's too stubborn; just refuses to."

Diem's death preceded Jack Kennedy's by just three weeks. What JFK would have done about American involvement in South Vietnam can never be known for certain. It is probable that not even he was sure.

Ken O'Donnell has been the most vigorous advocate of the argument that the President was planning to liquidate the American stake right after the completion of the 1964 elections would have made it politically possible. The withdrawal of those thousand advisers, he said, was but a first step in that process. At the time the Joint Chiefs asked for an increase of American strength to seventeen thousand, Kennedy told his military aide, Ted Clifton, that he would go along with the request but had warned that he would approve no more.

At that moment Kennedy could not have anticipated the shape of either the dramatic political climate or the situation in Southeast Asia. Still, for him to have withdrawn at any point short of a clear-cut settlement would have been most unlikely. As Sorensen has said in an oral-history interview, Kennedy "did feel strongly that for better or worse, enthusiastic or unenthusiastic, we had to stay there until we left on terms other than a retreat or abandonment of our commitment." The remarks he had planned to deliver at the Trade Mart in Dallas on the afternoon of November 22 contained the following statement of purpose: "Our assistance to these nations can be painful, risky and costly, as is true in Southeast Asia today. But we dare not weary of the test." "I talked with him hundreds of times about Vietnam," said Dean Rusk, "and on no single occasion did he ever whisper any such thing to his own secretary of state." In addition, and what was more important, Rusk pointed out, was that a decision in 1963 to take troops out in 1965 following the election of 1964 "would have been a decision to have Americans in uniform in combat for domestic political reasons. No President can do that and live with it." When Ken O'Donnell was pressed about whether the President's decision to withdraw meant that he would have undertaken the escalation that followed in 1965, the position became qualified. Kennedy, said O'Donnell, had not faced the same level of North Vietnamese infiltration as did President Johnson, thereby implying that he, too, would have responded in a similar way under those conditions. As Bobby Kennedy later said, his brother had reached the point where he felt that South Vietnam was worth keeping for psychological and political reasons "more than anything else."

Chapter 21 THE AMERICAN UNIVERSITY SPEECH

President Kennedy's American University speech, delivered on June 10, 1963, is often cited as a major initiative to end the Cold War. Does it reveal a softening of Kennedy's staunch anti-Communism? How did the President propose to achieve world disarmament?

"There are few earthly things more beautiful than a university," wrote John Masefield, in his tribute to English universities—and his words are equally true today. He did not refer to spires and towers, to campus greens and ivied walls. He admired the splendid beauty of the university, he said, because it was "a place where those who hate ignorance may strive to know, where those who perceive truth may strive to make others see."

I have, therefore, chosen this time and this place to discuss a topic on which ignorance too often abounds and the truth is too rarely perceived—yet it is the most important topic on earth: world peace.

What kind of peace do I mean? What kind of peace do we seek? Not a Pax Americana enforced on the world by American weapons of war. Not the peace of the grave or the security of the slave. I am talking about genuine peace, the kind of peace

From *Public Papers Of The Presidents Of The United States . . . 1963*.

that makes life on earth worth living, the kind that enables men and nations to grow and to hope and to build a better life for their children—not merely peace for Americans but peace for all men and women—not merely peace in our time but peace for all time.

I speak of peace because of the new face of war. Total war makes no sense in an age when great powers can maintain large and relatively invulnerable nuclear forces and refuse to surrender without resort to those forces. It makes no sense in an age when a single nuclear weapon contains almost ten times the explosive force delivered by all of the allied air forces in the Second World War. It makes no sense in an age when the deadly poisons produced by a nuclear exchange would be carried by wind and water and soil and seed to the far corners of the globe and to generations yet unborn.

Today the expenditure of billions of dollars every year on weapons acquired for the purpose of making sure we never need to use them is essential to keeping the peace. But surely the acquisition of such idle stockpiles—which can only destroy and never create—is not the only, much less the most efficient, means of assuring peace.

I speak of peace, therefore, as the necessary rational end of rational men. I realize that the pursuit of peace is not as dramatic as the pursuit of war—and frequently the words of the pursuer fall on deaf ears. But we have no more urgent task.

Some say that it is useless to speak of world peace or world law or world disarmament—and that it will be useless until the leaders of the Soviet Union adopt a more enlightened attitude. I hope they do. I believe we can help them do it. But I also believe that we must reexamine our own attitude—as individuals and as a Nation—for our attitude is as essential as theirs. And every graduate of this school, every thoughtful citizen who despairs of war and wishes to bring peace, should begin by looking inward—by examining his own attitude toward the possibilities of peace, toward the Soviet Union, toward the course of the cold war and toward freedom and peace here at home.

First: Let us examine our attitude toward peace itself. Too many of us think it is impossible. To many think it unreal. But that is a dangerous, defeatist belief. It leads to the conclusion that war is inevitable—that man is doomed—that we are gripped by forces we cannot control.

We need not accept that view. Our problems are manmade—therefore, they can be solved by man. And man can be as big as he wants. No problem of human destiny is beyond human beings. Man's reason and spirit have often solved the seemingly unsolvable—and we believe they can do it again.

I am not referring to the absolute, infinite concept of universal peace and good will of which some fantasies and fanatics dream. I do not deny the value of hopes and dreams but we merely invite discouragement and incredulity by making that our only and immediate goal.

Let us focus instead on a more practical, more attainable peace—based not on a sudden revolution in human nature but on a gradual evolution in human institutions—on a series of concrete actions and effective agreements which are in the interest of all concerned. There is no single, simple key to this peace—no grand or magic formula to be adopted by one or two powers. Genuine peace must be the product of many nations, the sum of many acts. It must be dynamic, not static, changing to meet the challenge of each new generation. For peace is a process—a way of solving problems.

With such a peace, there will still be quarrels and conflicting interests, as there are within families and nations. World peace, like community peace, does not require that each man love his neighbor—it requires only that they live together in mutual tolerance, submitting their disputes to a just and peaceful settlement. And history teaches us that enmities between nations, as between individuals, do not last forever. However fixed our likes and dislikes may seem, the tide of time and events will often bring surprising changes in the relations between nations and neighbors.

So let us persevere. Peace need not be impracticable, and war need not be inevitable. By defining our goal more clearly, by making it seem more manageable and less remote, we can help all peoples to see it, to draw hope from it, and to move irresistably toward it.

Second: Let us reexamine our attitude toward the Soviet Union. It is discouraging to think that their leaders may actually believe what their propagandists write. It is discouraging to read a recent authoritative Soviet text on *Military Strategy* and find, on page after page, wholly baseless and incredible claims—such as the allegation that "American imperialist circles are preparing to unleash different types of wars . . . that there is a very real threat of a preventive war being unleashed by American imperialists against the Soviet Union . . . [and that] the political aims of the American imperialists are to enslave economically and politically the European and other capitalist countries . . . [and] to achieve world domination . . . by means of aggressive wars."

Truly, as it was written long ago: "The wicked flee when no man pursueth." Yet it is sad to read these Soviet statements—to realize the extent of the gulf between us. But it is also a warning—a warning to the American people not to fall into the same trap of the Soviets, not to see only a distorted and desperate view of the other side, not to see conflict as inevitable, accommodation as impossible, and communication as nothing more than an exchange of threats.

No government or social system is so evil that its people must be considered as lacking in virtue. As Americans, we find communism profoundly repugnant as a negation of personal freedom and dignity. But we can still hail the Russian people for their many achievements—in science and space, in economic and industrial growth, in culture and in acts of courage.

Among the many traits the peoples of our two countries have in common, none is stronger than our mutual abhorrence of war. Almost unique, among the major world powers, we have never been at war with each other. And no nation in the history of battle ever suffered more than the Soviet Union suffered in the course of the Second World War. At least 20 million lost their lives. Countless millions of homes and farms were burned or sacked. A third of the nations's territory, including nearly two thirds of its industrial base, was turned into a wasteland—a loss equivalent to the devastation of this country east of Chicago.

Today, should total war ever break out again—no matter how—our two countries would become the primary targets. It is an ironic but accurate fact that the two strongest powers are the two in the most danger of devastation. All we have built, all we have worked for, would be destroyed in the first 24 hours. And even in the cold war, which brings burdens and dangers to so many countries, including this Nation's closest allies—our two countries bear the heaviest burdens. For we are both devoting massive sums of money to weapons that could be better devoted to combating ignorance, poverty, and disease. We are both caught up in a vicious and dangerous cycle in which suspicion on one side breeds suspicion on the other, and new weapons beget counterweapons.

In short, both the United States and its allies, and the Soviet Union and its allies, have a mutually deep interest in a just and genuine peace and in halting the arms race. Agreements to this end are in the interests of the Soviet Union as well as ours—and even the most hostile nations can be relied upon to accept and keep those treaty obligations, which are in their own interests.

So, let us not be blind to our differences—but let us also direct attention to our common interests and to the means by which those differences can be resolved. And if we cannot end now our differences, at least we can help make the world safe for diversity. For, in the final analysis, our most basic common link is that we all inhabit this small planet. We all breathe the same air. We all cherish our children's future. And we are all mortal.

Third: Let us reexamine our attitude toward the cold war, remembering that we are not engaged in a debate, seeking to pile up debating points. We are not here distributing blame or pointing the finger of judgment. We must deal with the world as it is, and not as it might have been had the history of the last 18 years been different.

We must, therefore, persevere in the search for peace in the hope that constructive changes within the Communist bloc might bring within reach solutions which now seem beyond us. We must conduct our affairs in such a way that it becomes in the Communists' interest to agree on a genuine peace. Above all, while defending our own vital interests, nuclear powers must avert those confrontations which bring an adversary to a choice of either a humiliating retreat or a nuclear war. To adopt that kind of course in the nuclear age would be evidence only of the bankruptcy of our policy— or of a collective death-wish for the world.

To secure these ends, America's weapons are nonprovocative, carefully controlled, designed to deter, and capable of selective use. Our military forces are committed to peace and disciplined in self-restraint. Our diplomats are instructed to avoid unnecessary irritants and purely rhetorical hostility.

For we can seek a relaxation of tensions without relaxing our guard. And, for our part, we do not need to use threats to prove that we are resolute. We do not need to jam foreign broadcasts out of fear our faith will be eroded. We are unwilling to impose our system on any unwilling people—but we are willing and able to engage in peaceful competition with any people on earth.

Meanwhile, we seek to strengthen the United Nations, to help solve its financial problems, to make it a more effective instrument for peace, to develop it into a genuine world security system—a system capable of resolving disputes on the basis of law, of insuring the security of the large and the small, and of creating conditions under which arms can finally be abolished.

At the same time we seek to keep peace inside the non-Communist world, where many nations, all of them our friends, are divided over issues which weaken Western unity, which invite Communist intervention or which threaten to erupt into war. Our efforts in West New Guinea, in the Congo, in the Middle East, and in the Indian subcontinent, have been persistent and patient despite criticism from both sides. We have also tried to set an example for others—by seeking to adjust small but significant differences with our own closest neighbors in Mexico and in Canada.

Speaking of others nations, I wish to make one point clear. We are bound to many nations by alliances. Those alliances exist because our concern and theirs substantially overlap. Our commitment to defend Western Europe and West Berlin, for example, stands undiminished because of the identity of our vital interests. The United States will make no deal with the Soviet Union at the expense of other nations and other peoples, not merely because they are our partners, but also because their interests and ours converge.

Our interests converge, however, not only in defending the frontiers of freedom, but in pursuing the paths of peace. It is our hope—and the purpose of allied policies—to convince the Soviet Union that she, too should let each nation choose its own future, so long as that choice does not interfere with the choices of others. The Communist drive to impose their political and economic system on others is the primary cause of world tension today. For there can be no doubt that, if all nations could refrain from interfering in the self-determination of others, the peace would be much more assured.

This will require a new effort to achieve world law—a new context for world discussions. It will require increased understanding between the Soviets and ourselves. And increased understanding will require increased contact and communication. One step in this direction is the proposed arrangement for a direct line between Moscow and Washington, to avoid on each side of the dangerous delays, misunderstandings, and misreadings of the other's actions which might occur at a time of crisis.

We have also been talking in Geneva about other first-step measures of arms control, designed to limit the intensity of the arms race and to reduce the risks of accidental war. Our primary long-range interest in Geneva, however, is general and complete disarmament—designed to take place by stages, permitting parallel political developments to build the new institutions of peace which would take the place of arms. The pursuit of disarmament has been an effort of this Government since the 1920's. It has been urgently sought by the past three administrations. And however dim the respects may be today, we intend to continue this effort—to continue it in order that all countries, including our own, can better grasp what the problems and possibilities of disarmament are.

The one major area of these negotiations where the end is in sight, yet where a fresh start is badly needed, is in a treaty to outlaw nuclear tests. The conclusion of such a treaty, so near and yet so far, would check the spiraling arms race in one of its most dangerous areas. It would place the nuclear powers in a position to deal more effectively with one of the greatest hazards which man faces in 1963, the further spread of nuclear arms. It would increase our security—it would decrease the prospects of war. Surely this goal is sufficiently important to require our steady pursuit, yielding neither to the temptation to give up the whole effort nor the temptation to give up our insistence on vital and responsible safeguards.

I am taking this opportunity, therefore, to announce two important decisions in this regard.

First: Chairman Khrushchev, Prime Minister Macmillan, and I have agreed that high-level discussions will shortly begin in Moscow looking toward early agreement on a comprehensive test ban treaty. Our hopes must be tempered with the caution of history—but with our hopes go the hopes of all mankind.

Second: To make clear our good faith and solemn convictions on the matter, I now declare that the United States does not propose to conduct nuclear tests in the atmosphere so long as other states do not do so. We will not be the first to resume. Such a declaration is no substitute for a formal binding treaty, but I hope it will help us achieve one. Nor would such a treaty be a substitute for disarmament, but I hope it will help us achieve it.

Finally, my fellow Americans, let us examine our attitude toward peace and freedom here at home. The quality and spirit of our own society must justify and support our efforts abroad. We must show it in the dedication of our own lives—as many of you who are graduating today will have a unique opportunity to do, by serving without pay in the Peace Corps abroad or in the proposed National Service Corps here at home.

But wherever we are, we must all, in our daily lives, live up to the age-old faith that peace and freedom walk together. In too many of our cities today, the peace is not secure because freedom is incomplete.

It is the responsibility of the executive branch at all levels of government—local, State, and National—to provide and protect that freedom for all of our citizens by all means within their authority. It is the responsibility of the legislative branch at all levels, wherever the authority is not now adequate, to make it adequate. And it is the responsibility of all citizens in all sections of this country to respect the rights of all others and to respect the law of the land.

All this is not unrelated to world peace. "When a man's ways please the Lord," the Scriptures tell us, "he maketh even his enemies to be at peace with him." And is not peace, in the last analysis, basically a matter of human right—the right to live out our lives without fear of devastation—the right to breathe air as nature provided it—the right of future generations to a healthy existence?

While we proceed to safeguard our national interests, let us also safeguard human interests. And the elimination of war and arms is clearly in the interest of both. No treaty, however much it may be to the advantage of all, however tightly it may be worded, can provide absolute security against the risks of deception and evasion. But it can—if it is sufficiently effective in its enforcement and if it is sufficiently in the interests of its signers—offer far more security and far fewer risks than an unabated, uncontrolled, unpredictable arms race.

The United States, as the world knows, will never start a war. We do not want a war. We do not now expect a war. This generation of Americans has already had enough—more than enough—of war and hate and oppression. We shall be prepared if others wish it. We shall be alert to try to stop it. But we shall also do our part to build a world of peace where the weak are safe and the strong are just. We are not helpless before that task or hopeless of its success. Confident and unafraid, we labor on—not toward a strategy of annihilation but toward a strategy of peace.

Part Six

THE LEGACY

Chapter 22 AN ARDENT COLD WARRIOR

THOMAS G. PATERSON (b. 1941) is a professor of history at the University of Connecticut. He has written extensively on the Cold
War. This assessment of JFK's achievements
was designed for the twentieth anniversary of
Kennedy's assassination. Does Paterson under-
estimate the importance of the American University speech?

The assassination of John F. Kennedy left us wondering: Would he have improved
upon his record had he lived? Would he have tamed the cold war, withdrawn from
Vietnam, and slowed the military buildup?

Kennedy's admirers have asked us not to judge him by his limited accomplishments, but by his intentions, for, had he lived, he would have done better. But
historians can only report on what he actually did in office, not on what he might have
done. And even speculation proves disappointing, because there is scant evidence that
he would have reversed the nuclear arms race, turned around in Vietnam, opened
relations with the People's Republic of China, or effected detente with Russia.

The president was an ardent cold warrior whose personal style of toughness and
reading of lessons from the 1940s propelled him into a multitude of crises.

His June 1963 American University speech, in which he called for negotiations

"JFK's Achievements Were Really Limited," *USA Today*, November 22, 1983, p. 8A.

with the Soviets, is often cited as his change of heart, his shedding of inherited cold war wisdom. But as former ambassador George F. Kennedy remarked, one speech is not enough.

Kennedy and his aides swept into Washington ready to launch a bold, activist foreign policy to win the cold war and woo the Third World.

They were, said a skeptical undersecretary of state Chester Bowles, "sort of looking for the chance to prove their muscle." Adlai Stevenson soon became disenchanted: "They've got the damndest bunch of boy commandos running around . . . you ever saw."

Kennedy leaned heavily upon military solutions. The Peace Corps and the Alliance for Progress were put in place, to be sure. But military policies predominated—at the Bay of Pigs, during the Berlin Crisis, and in Vietnam. He ordered more than 16,000 "advisers" to Vietnam and increased military aid to the Diem regime.

Privately, he told a few doves that he intended to withdraw from Vietnam after the 1964 election, but all of his decisions escalated intervention and many of his assistants stayed on to help drive Lyndon Johnson deeper into a war that could not be won.

Even though Kennedy knew that the missile gap he had harped upon in the 1960 campaign did not exist, he nonetheless increased the defense budget by 15 percent in his first year, and greatly expanded the nuclear arsenal.

If the defense of Kennedy's hawkishness is that right-wingers pushed him to go to the brink, then we must reply that we would have preferred a statesman to a politician who played to dangerous opinion.

No, it is Kennedy's own ingrained cold warriorism that we must emphasize. Troubled by it, unable to shed it, he shaped his policies to satisfy it.

Chapter 23 THE UNPRINCIPLED

MIDGE DECTER (b. 1927) is a well-known writer and editor. A neoconservative, she is critical of the Kennedy Administration for its alleged arrogance and lack of principle. Was JFK merely "an avid reader of the temper of the times"? What did "ideas" mean, in Decter's judgment, to the New Frontiersmen?

The truly interesting question about the Kennedy administration, though, is not what did it accomplish but what, in the words of Oscar Gass, "did these people want."

For besides elegance and gaiety, that which preeminently characterized the New Frontier was a kind of swashbuckling, an arrogant lack of principle. By "lack of principle" I do not mean that anybody was an especially unprincipled individual. Anyway, only children or idlers level such charges at political leaders. What I do mean is that Kennedy and his "best and brightest people in the country" swooped down on the White House and tackled its problems in the spirit of the belief that these problems continued to persist only because the "right" people had never before been let loose on them. How much there was to be undone and cleared away: the work of Truman hacks and Eisenhower dullards, an inert State Department, not very bright generals, a bunch of small-time tacky Congressmen. And who could conceivably be better for the job? This spirit accounts in part, probably in great part, for the enormous new elan they brought to Washington. ". . . They aspired," Schlesinger tells us, "like their President, to the world of ideas as well as the world of power." "Ideas," in Kennedy parlance, meant proposals for programs to initiate—a perfect technocratic definition of the term—and if there was a distinction to be made in anybody's mind between a new proposal and a genuinely new policy, Schlesinger, who normally does understand such a distinction, gives no indication of it. . . . The Alliance for Progress—the adaptation of a new posture and a new rhetoric to Point Four—serves as a notable example of one such program; the Peace Corps serves as another—a genuinely original but hardly earth-shattering move in the same direction as above; and a third, painful at the moment to mention, was the tooling up of the American military for counter-insurgency warfare.

Lack of respect for, lack of imagination of, the genuine difficulties—and yes, even the genuine convictions—of one's failed predecessors is the first mark of what I have termed arrogant lack of principle. Its base lies perhaps in snobbishness, perhaps in a parochial lack of that curiosity which for educated men spells cultivation of spirit, certainly in a hunger for power that can be fluidly and comfortably wielded. Among other things, the New Frontiersmen swept through the offices of duly elected representatives of the people—some of them duly elected and reelected for nearly as many years as theirs interlocutors had been alive—and with a tough-minded political-science knowledge of the low calling of the legislator, made a shambles of White House-Congressional relations.

The other side of the swashbuckling was a deadly caution. Nor was caution a contradiction, but rather in the fullest sense a complement, of New Frontier auto-intoxication. Any possibility for a greatness of record, as distinguishable from high style and intention, Kennedy avoided. He took no real leadership except in foreign policy, and even there it was largely a matter of making a personal impression and establishing personal relations. He was instead an avid reader of the temper of the times. In some cases he badly misread that temper—for example, the degree of impatience among Negroes with the pace of progress in civil rights and the degree of impatience in the country at large with anti-Communism as a guiding principle of foreign policy—and lost opportunities already prepared for him. He had attained the White House by the narrowest margin and naturally wanted to stay there through his allotted eight years. What tiny margin of popularity he had, had followed on a campaign in which the major stated issue between him and his opponent was that he was the better man, that he would "get the country moving again." His mandate was thus undefined, and he set out to fulfill it, as he incomparably did, exactly as promised: by being the better man. And his New Frontiersmen in turn set out to fulfill their mandate from him by constituting themselves, throughout the Executive, a group appearing to be the most dashing and creative public officials ever. Here, indeed, was where the fun lay, for all of them, and directly and indirectly, for the rest of the country.

What the Kennedy administration wanted, then, what it sought to do, was to impose an image of itself on American society and American history: an image of itself as the rightful, by virtue of intrinsic superiority, American ruling class. And in this endeavor it was unquestionably successful.

Chapter 24 THE INCARNATION OF AN ERA

DAVID E. KAISER (b. 1947) teaches history
at Carnegie-Mellon University and specializes
in recent American political history. Here he
presents a positive assessment of the New
Frontier, both in domestic affairs and foreign
relations. Why, in Kaiser's view, was JFK "the
incarnation of an era"?

As President, Kennedy disappointed liberals by his failure to push their agenda of aid
to education, Medicare, and civil rights more effectively, but he probably had a better
sense of the mood of the country than they. Despite large Democratic majorities in
Congress, key committees remained firmly in the hands of Southern conservatives.
Kennedy shrewdly husbanded his political capital until faced with a true national
crisis: the problem of civil rights.

The President contributed only indirectly to the growth of the civil rights move-
ment. His own views were distinctly ambivalent. Confronted with the problem of
African ambassadors who were forbidden to eat at roadside restaurants between New
York and Washington, he suggested that they fly. In the spring of 1961 Attorney
General Robert Kennedy asked freedom riders to call off their campaign because "the
President is going abroad, and this is all embarrassing him." Yet J.F.K.'s rhetorical

From "The Politician," *The New Republic*, 189 (November 21, 1983), 18–19, by permission.

commitment to freedom for all Americans inspired demonstrators, both white and black to try to make his words come true. The sit-in movement spread rapidly through the South, leading to a near-revolution in Birmingham, Alabama, in the spring of 1963. Then Kennedy responded—both because of a gradual change in his own views, and because a constituency for dramatic steps had emerged.

It was Kennedy, not Lyndon Johnson, who in 1963 introduced sweeping civil rights legislation designed to deal with education, voting rights, employment discrimination, and above all with exclusion from public accommodations. And although Johnson's unparalleled legislative skill eased the bill's passage in 1964, it almost certainly would have passed under Kennedy as well. At the time of his death a redrawn bill was nearing House passage, and in the Senate the key contact—with Republican leader Everett Dirksen, whose support could stop a Southern filibuster—had already been established.

Kennedy's contribution to the end of legal discrimination in the South was his major domestic achievement. And although his civil rights stance cost him some popularity points, his Gallup poll rating still stood at 59 percent shortly before his death—higher than any other postwar President at the same stage of his term except Eisenhower. Had he lived he would certainly have defeated Goldwater.

In foreign affairs Kennedy's Presidency is widely viewed as the apotheosis of the cold war, but here, too, his views evolved as circumstances changed. Certainly his 1960 campaign rhetoric and his inaugural address focused on Soviet-American confrontation and competition. Given the temper of the times this was inevitable. Neither Nixon nor any of the other Democratic candidates took an appreciably different view of the world situation: the Soviets had determined to conquer the world, and only we could stop them. Newly independent nations were an especially crucial battleground, and it was not only right but necessary that they follow the American path. In his first year in office, faced with Khrushchev's threats over Berlin, Kennedy took the possibility of all-out war seriously. He approved a massive strategic arms buildup even after discovering that the "missile gap" did not exist, built up conventional forces, and encouraged the construction of bomb shelters. Soviet-American relations did not improve during Kennedy's first two years in office.

Events moved more swiftly in the third world. Here Kennedy pursued a coherent, two-pronged policy: a no-holds-barred struggle against Communist-influenced regimes or forces, and an attempt to build up non-Communist democratic alternatives. Like Kennedy's rhetoric, his extralegal forays in the third world were not original. Both the Bay of Pigs invasion and the plans to assassinate Castro stemmed from the Eisenhower Administration, and the latter continued into the Johnson years. And though Kennedy pursued such plans with gusto, he coupled them with sincere efforts to promote democracy. In Latin America, in the Congo, and even in Vietnam, he painstakingly sought non-Communist democratic alternatives. The frequent failures of this policy reflected the weakness of the assumptions behind it. The dilemmas it faced still bedevil American policy in Central America and elsewhere. Kennedy's charm was as useful in dealing with the third world as it was at home, if not more so. New nations never forgot that in 1957 he was the first American statesman to call for independence for Algeria, and no other President has approached his popularity among the leaders and the people of less-developed nations.

Kennedy's handling of the Cuban missile crisis must also be evaluated in light of political realities. We can now appreciate that, as Robert McNamara pointed out then, the new Soviet missiles in Cuba would not have drastically affected the strategic balance. But this consideration must be weighed against the political reality of 1962. During the crisis Kennedy continually faced pressure from the military and from powerful legislators to take stronger action, not weaker. To solve the crisis he had to evade this pressure. On Saturday, October 27, with an invasion of Cuba only forty-eight hours away, Robert Kennedy saw Soviet Ambassador Dobrynin. Publicly Kennedy could not trade U.S. missiles in Turkey for a Soviet withdrawal; such a step would have been labeled another Munich and destroyed his effectiveness. Privately, however, Robert Kennedy told Dobrynin that while there could be no question of a public deal, within a short time the Turkish missiles would be gone. Khrushchev annouced the withdrawal of Soviet missiles from Cuba the next day.

Subsequently Kennedy dramatically eased Soviet-American tensions. His speech at American University on June 10, 1963, signaled a move away from the cold war. (Those who regard Kennedy as an arch-cold warrior might ponder how astonishing, and welcome, it would be to hear such a speech come out of the White House today.) The Administration negotiated the Test Ban Treaty, prevailed upon the Joint Chiefs to testify in its favor, and shepherded it through the Senate. With Kennedy's help, the vision of a death struggle with the Soviet Union quickly faded from American consciousness—a change confirmed by Goldwater's crushing 1964 defeat.

Whether a further re-evaluation of the cold war might have avoided the catastrophe of Vietnam remains the great unanswerable question of Kennedy's Presidency. For three years he tried to to save South Vietnam without an American combat troop commitment. Had he lived, Kennedy, like Johnson, would have been faced with a choice between a total collapse of South Vietnam and a full-scale, open-ended, long-term commitment of American troops. His dovish comments to Mike Mansfield and Wayne Morse do not prove what he would have done, but they show a more flexible view than that of his successor. Political considerations would have inclined him against such a commitment at the outset of his second term, or against escalating U.S. troop involvement when its unpopularity became apparent. Perhaps he could have dealt with the painful lesson of our inability to achieve our aims at any remotely acceptable cost more effectively than did Johnson and Nixon. He could hardly have done worse.

Kennedy remains a significant historical figure because he was, for better or for worse, the incarnation of an era. In his time he and almost all Americans believed passionately in an American mission to secure liberty both at home and abroad, and in a need to demonstrate both the superiority of our system and the justice of our cause.

The Peace Corps and the space program are perhaps the most appropriate symbols of his Presidency. They expressed our eagerness to show the way to new nations and to master exciting new technology. The missions who gathered around their television sets to watch the launchings from Cape Canaveral thrived on their country's efforts to match and surpass Soviet achievements, and shared the excitement of a new age.

Chapter 25 **KENNEDY AS MYTH**

The eminent American historian WILLIAM
E. LEUCHTENBURG (b. 1922) is a professor
of history at the University of North Carolina.
In this essay, Leuchtenburg argues that Kennedy "has become myth." What precisely
does this mean? Are historians truly unable to
create an accurate picture of JFK and judge
his activities?

The murder of John F. Kennedy . . . occasioned an overwhelming sense of grief that
may be without parallel in our history. When the news first was announced, people
wept openly in the streets, and during the painful weekend that followed, as the
mesmerizing images of the youthful President and his family were flashed again and
again on the television screens, the feeling of deprivation deepened. A San Francisco
columnist reported: "It is less than 72 hours since the shots rang out in Dallas, yet it
seems a lifetime—a lifetime of weeping skies, wet eyes and streets. . . . Over the
endless weekend, San Francisco looked liked a city that was only slowly emerging
from a terrible bombardment. Downtown, on what would normally have been a
bustling Saturday, the people walked slowly, as in shock, their faces pale and drawn,
their mood as somber as the dark clothes they wore under the gray skies."

From "John F. Kennedy, Twenty Years Later," by William E. Leuchtenburg, *American Heritage*, 35
(December, 1983), 51–3, 57–9.

To the slain President's admirers and associates, his death signified not merely a cruel personal loss but the end of an era. "For all of us, life goes on—but brightness has fallen from the air," observed his special counsel Theodore Sorensen. "A Golden age is over and it will never be again." One of Kennedy's earliest biographers, William Manchester, had jotted down on the morning of Kennedy's Inauguration the words of the sixteenth-century martyr, Hugh Latimer. "We shall this day light such a candle by God's grace . . . as I trust shall never be put out." "Now," Manchester wrote, "the light was gone from our lives, and I was left to grope in the darkness of the dead past." At the United Nations, Adlai Stevenson rose to say, "We will bear the grief of his death to the day of ours."

Yet the mourning for Kennedy was by no means limited to his circle; it was felt no less deeply by those who had been his critics and adversaries. . . . In Guinea, Sekou Toure stated, "I have lost my only true friend in the outside world," and in Algiers, Ben Bella, his voice breaking, said, "I can't believe it. Believe me, I'd rather it happen to me than to him."

Such expressions were not atypical but representative, for the most conspicuous aspect of the anguish over the assassination was its worldwide character. In London more than a thousand traveled from distant parts of the city to pay homage at the U.S. Embassy in Grosvenor Square, and the same instinct drew mourners to the American missions in Moscow and in Cairo, in Madras and in Tananarive. On the hillsides in Kampala by the residence of the American envoy, Ugandans sat in a silent vigil. From Yokohama a correspondent wrote: "Immediately when there came the news of Mr. Kennedy's death, there was a silencing of life here and then a siege of grief as I have never seen before and never thought possible in Japan. No one told the Japanese to be shocked: they just cried with pain and anger and sorrow, as if the human psyche had been slammed in a car door, and maimed."

In Britain the BBC's "That Was The Week That Was," a program distinguished by its impiety toward authority, called Kennedy "the first Western politician to make politics a respectable profession in thirty years," and in the *Manchester Guardian Weekly*, David Gourlay went so far as to say, "For the first time in my life I think I know how the disciples must have felt when Jesus was crucified."

In the United States historians were not immune from such sentiments, though they were inclined to be more restrained. Even in 1963 they were reluctant to subscribe to the sentiment revealed by *Public Opinion Quarterly*, which found that "a full half of the adult population" in America judged Kennedy to be "one of the two or three best Presidents the country ever had." Yet a good many historians were disposed to give him good marks. James MacGregor Burns, who had taken a detached view of Kennedy in his exemplary campaign biography, concluded that, as a dramatizer of issues, Kennedy rated with Lincoln, while Arthur Link, author of the definitive multivolume life of Woodrow Wilson, observed that Kennedy brought to the White House "qualities of vigor, rationality, and noble vision matched only by Theodore Roosevelt, Woodrow Wilson, and Franklin Roosevelt in this century. It is too early to try to fix his place among the Presidents, but I am inclined to believe that historians will rank him as a great President."

Today, twenty years afterward, historians are far from reaching a consensus on President Kennedy, but few would be disposed to rank him so highly. The imagery associated with the name *Kennedy*, so brightly burnished in 1963, has tarnished; to bring to mind the episodes that caused dismay requires only the evocation of certain code words: Onassis, Chappaquiddick, Judith Exner. Kennedy's reputation has been deflated by what one writer called "a group of late-souring historians known collectively as revisionists," and even those who had once been well disposed toward him have had second thoughts. Asked in 1973 whether his view of Kennedy had changed in the past decade, Arthur Link replied: "I should say that I somewhat overrated his abilities, his vision. . . . As we look back on the years '61 to '63, what seemed like great events and forward movement don't seem so great and so forward now." . . .

Perhaps the most judicious appreciation of Kennedy has come from a man who might have been expected to have been a critic, the socialist Michael Harrington, who said in 1973: "The claim I make for his historic significance is both restrained and major. Within the limits of the possible, as defined by his own pragmatic liberalism and the reactionary congressional power arrayed against it, he developed to a surprising degree. How far he would have gone, we will never know. (Robert Kennedy, who survived his brother by a little less than five years, spent them in making the most extraordinary pilgrimage a practicing politician has ever traveled. What if John Kennedy had had those years too?) John F. Kennedy . . . must be judged not as a shining knight nor as a failed hero but as a man of his time and place. . . . He was not, of course, a radical and it is silly to accuse him, as some of his disillusioned followers have, of not having carried out basic transformations of the system. That was never his intention and had it been the people would not have elected him President.

"And yet, within the context of his political and personal limitations, John F. Kennedy grew enormously. He arrived at the White House a young, and not terribly distinguished, senator from the Eisenhower years with a tiny margin of victory and a Dixiecrat-Republican majority against him in the Congress.

"The America which inaugurated him in January, 1961, still believed in the verities of the Cold War (as did Kennedy in his speech of that day), in the sanctity of the balanced budget, and it had not begun to come to terms with that great mass movement led by Martin Luther King, Jr. The America which mourned John F. Kennedy in November, 1963, was different. It was not transformed—but it was better. That was Kennedy's modest and magnificent achievement."

In the years to come, historians, while continuing to refine their estimates of Kennedy, will probably conclude that there is more to the history of this time than deciding whether Kennedy deserves to be admitted to the Valhalla of "Great Presidents," assigned to the vestibule of the "near great" or shoved into more crowded quarters with all the rest.

The subject invites the attention of the social historian and the cultural historian.

William Carleton has reflected on Kennedy as a romantic hero: "Strange that he should have come out of the America of the machine and mass production. Or is it? People in our prosaic age, particularly young Americans, were yearning for a romantic hero, as the James Dean cult among our youth reveals. Now they have an authentic one." Mark Gelfand, an authority on the history of the city, has pointed out that Kennedy was the spokesman of postindustrial America, of a metropolitan sophistication far removed from the sensibility of an Al Smith. (When Kennedy first ran for office, an observer noted with astonishment that "he never even went to a wake unless he knew the deceased personally.") Kennedy, the critic David Bazelon has written, succeeded in "ridding us at last of Abe's log cabin . . . and allowing us to enter a twentieth-century fantasy with city immigrants as heroes, instead of homesteading farmers." . . .

However, in the end the efforts of the historians are not likely to have a very considerable effect on Kennedy's reputation, for he has already become part not of history but of myth, a myth that much of the public embraced and historians could not altogether escape. As Theodore White has observed: "More than any other President since Lincoln, John F. Kennedy has become myth. The greatest President in the stretch between them was, of course, Franklin D. Roosevelt; but it was difficult to make myth of Franklin Roosevelt, the country squire, the friendly judge, the approachable politician, the father figure. Roosevelt was a great man because he understood his times, and because almost always, at the historic intersections, he took the fork in the road that proved to be correct. He was so right and so strong, it was sport to challenge him. But Kennedy was cut off at the promise, not after the performance, and so it was left to television and his widow, Jacqueline, to frame the man as legend." The legend did not take long to evolve. By the time of the first anniversary of his death, *Newsweek* was remarking, "In the bare space of a year . . . Mr. Kennedy had been transfigured from man into myth—an enshrinement that would have pained him to see," and the columnist James Reston concluded, "Deprived of the place he sought in history, he has been given in compensation a place in legend."

The mythmakers focused on Kennedy as romantic hero, in part because Kennedy sometimes perceived himself in this manner. After his death his widow remarked: "Once . . . I thought history was something that bitter old men wrote. But then I realized history made Jack what he was. You must think of him as this little boy, sick so much of the time, reading in bed, reading history, reading the Knights of the Round Table, reading Marlborough. For Jack, history was full of heroes." In his very first race for Congress in 1946, Kennedy would tell his boon companion Dave Powers: "Years from now you can say you were with me on Saint Crispin's Day. We few, we happy few, we band of brothers." Perhaps not everything that Powers remembers occurred quite as he recounts it, but the story gains credence from the fact that Kennedy did know the Saint Crispin's Day passage from Shakespeare's *Henry V* by heart, and during a performance by Basil Rathbone at the White House, the President's only request was for that speech. Benjamin Bradlee noted that he "had a Walter

Mitty streak in him, as wide as his smile. On the golf course, when he was winning, he reminded himself most of Arnold Palmer in raw power, or Julius Boros in finesse. When he was losing, he was 'the old warrior' at the end of a brilliant career, asking only that his faithful caddy point him in the right direction, and let instinct take over."

The chivalric imagery was fostered, too, by his survivors, especially by his widow. The mode was set by the elaborate state funeral that she arranged—the riderless charger with reserved boots, the tolling bells, the relentless rolls of the drums, the Black Watch Pipers, the queen of Greece and the king of the Belgians and the emperor of Ethiopia and the majestic Charles de Gaulle striding up Connecticut Avenue, and, finally, as the cortege ended its long journey, Jacqueline bending with a torch to light the eternal flame. "It was a day," wrote Mary McGrory, "of such endless fitness, with so much pathos and panoply, so much grief nobly borne."

As important as this occasion was in establishing the romantic legend, Jacqueline Kennedy contributed even more in a subsequent interview with Theodore White. She told him: "At night, before we'd go to sleep, Jack liked to play some records; and the song he loved most came at the very end of this record. The lines he loved to hear were: *"Don't let it be forgot, that once there was a spot, for one brief shining moment that was known as Camelot."* She emphasized: "There'll be great Presidents again—and the Johnsons are wonderful, they've been wonderful to me—but there'll never be another Camelot again." The rubric *Camelot* quickly made its way into the historical literature. Indeed, Samuel Eliot Morison ended his 1965 chronicle *The Oxford History of the American people* with the lyrics from the Loewe-Lerner musical, including the words: "That once there was a fleeting wisp of glory—called Camelot."

It is unlikely that historians will ever again give so much credence to the conception of Camelot, but Kennedy's place in our history as the romantic hero, cruelly slain in his prime, seems secure. As the columnist Gerald Johnson observed: "Logical analysis will certainly be applied to Kennedy's career, and will have about as much effect on his position in history as Mrs. Partington's mop had upon the Atlantic tide. . . . Historians may protest, logicians may rave, but they cannot alter the fact that any kind of man, once touched by romance, is removed from all categories and is comparable only with the legendary. . . . Already it has happened to two of the 35 men who have held the Presidency, rendering them incapable of analysis by the instruments of scholarship; and now Washington, the god-like, and Lincoln, the saintly, have been joined by Kennedy, the young Chevalier."

Like the fair youth on Keats's Grecian urn, Kennedy will be forever in pursuit, forever unfulfilled, but also "for ever young," beyond the power of time and the words of historians.

SUGGESTIONS FOR FURTHER READING

For favorable surveys of the Kennedy family history, see Joseph Dinneen, *The Kennedy Family* (Boston, 1959), Joseph W. McCarthy, *The Remarkable Kennedys* (New York, 1960), and Doris Kearns Goodwin, *The Fitzgeralds And The Kennedys* (New York, 1987). More critical and accurate accounts are in Peter Collier and David Horowitz, *The Kennedys, An American Drama* (New York, 1984), John H. Davis, *The Kennedys: Dynasty And Disaster, 1848–1983* (New York, 1984), and Thomas C. Reeves, *A Question Of Character: The Life Of John F. Kennedy* (New York, 1990). See also Harrison Rainie and John Quinn, *Growing Up Kennedy* (New York, 1983). The Kennedys are sharply criticized in Nancy Gager Clinch, *The Kennedy Neurosis: A Psychological Portrait Of An American Dynasty* (New York, 1973) and Gary Wills, *The Kennedy Imprisonment: A Meditation On Power* (Boston, 1981).

The best biographies of Joseph P. Kennedy are Richard J. Whalen, *The Founding Father, The Story Of Joseph P. Kennedy* (New York, 1964), and David E. Koskoff, *Joseph P. Kennedy, A Life And Times* (Englewood Cliffs, New Jersey, 1974). Materials from the long-concealed Joseph P. Kennedy Papers are in Goodwin, *The Fitzgeralds And The Kennedys*. Michael R. Beschloss's *Kennedy And Roosevelt, The Uneasy Alliance* (New York, 1980) is first-rate scholarship. See William J. Duncliffe, *The Life And Times Of Joseph P. Kennedy* (New York, 1965) and the worshipful Edward M. Kennedy (ed.), *The Fruitful Bough: A Tribute To Joseph P. Kennedy* (privately printed, 1965). See also Gloria Swanson, *Swanson On Swanson* (New York, 1980) for the silent screen star's memories. Rita Dallas and Jeanira Ratcliffe, *The Kennedy Case* (New York, 1973) and Frank Saunders, *Torn Lace Curtain* (New York, 1982) contain highly revealing recollections of the elder Kennedy.

For a glowing biography of Mrs. Kennedy, see Gail Cameron, *Rose: A Biography Of Rose Fitzgerald Kennedy* (New York, 1971). Rose Fitzgerald Kennedy, *Times To Remember* (Garden City, New York, 1974) is an often less than candid autobiography. See also Barbara Gibson and Caroline Latham, *Life With Rose Kennedy* (New York, 1986) and Saunders' valuable *Torn Lace Curtain*.

Much of the JFK legend may be found in James MacGregor Burns, *John Kennedy: A Political Profile* (New York, 1959), Theodore H. White, *The Making Of The President, 1960* (New York, 1961), Joan Meyers (ed.), *John Fitzgerald Kennedy . . . As We Remember Him* (New York, 1965). Kenneth P. O'Donnell and David F. Powers, *"Johnny, We Hardly Knew Ye," Memories Of John Fitzgerald Kennedy* (Boston, 1970), and William Manchester, *One Brief Shining Moment: Remembering Kennedy* (Boston, 1983). See also Paul B. Fay, Jr., *The Pleasure Of His Company* (New York, 1966).

For objective examinations of Kennedy's pre-White House years, see Joan and Clay Blair, Jr., *The Search For J.F.K.* (New York, 1976) and Herbert S. Parmet, *Jack: The Struggles Of John F. Kennedy* (New York, 1980). Robert J. Donovan, *PT 109: John F. Kennedy In World War II* (New York, 1961) and Richard Tresaskis, *John F. Kennedy And PT 109* (New York, 1962) are favorable interpretations of Kennedy's wartime activities. Ralph G. Martin and Ed Plaut, *Front Runner, Dark Horse* (Garden City, New York, 1960) contains important information on Kennedys's political campaigning.

The most accurate look at Jacqueline Kennedy is in Davis, *The Kennedys*. Mary Barelli Gallagher, *My Life With Jacqueline Kennedy* (New York, 1969) and J. B. West, *Upstairs At The White House, My Life With The First Ladies* (New York, 1973) are revealing. See also Letitia Baldrige, *Of Diamonds And Diplomats* (Boston, 1968). Stephen Birmingham's saccharine *Jacqueline Bouvier Kennedy Onassis* (New York, 1978) and Kitty Kelley's caustic *Jackie Oh!* (Secaucus, New Jersey, 1978) make an interesting contrast.

Several memoirs, beyond those already cited, shed light on JFK. Hubert H. Humphrey, *The Education Of A Public Man: My Life And Politics* (Garden City, New York, 1976) describes Kennedy campaign tactics in the 1960 primaries. See also volume one of Richard Nixon, *RN: The Memoirs Of Richard Nixon* (New York, 1978). Loyalist accounts of the White House years include Evelyn Lincoln, *My Twelve Years With John F. Kennedy* (New York, 1965), Maude Shaw, *White House Nannie* (New York, 1966), Janet Travell, *Office Hours: Day And Night* (New York, 1968), Pierre Salinger, *With Kennedy* (Garden City, New York, 1966), and Lawrence O'Brien, *No Final Victories: A Life In Politics—From John F. Kennedy To Watergate* (Garden City, New York, 1974).

Benjamin C. Bradlee, *Conversations With Kennedy* (New York, 1975) badly damaged the Kennedy mythology. Nancy Dickerson, *Among Those Present: A Reporter's View Of Twenty-five Years In Washington* (New York, 1976) and Traphes Bryant, *Dog Days At The White House* (New York, 1975) speak frankly of the dark side of the President's character. Judith Exner's *My Story* (New York, 1977) contains an explosive and believable portrait of the President by a favorite mistress. See also Walter Trohan, *Political Animals, Memoirs Of A Sentimental Cynic* (Garden City, New York, 1975), Bobby Baker, *Wheeling And Dealing: Confessions Of A Capitol Hill Operator* (New York, 1978), Tip O'Neill, *Man Of The House: The Life and Political Memoirs Of Speaker Tip O'Neill* (New York, 1987), and Oleg Cassini, *In My Own Fashion, An Autobiography* (New York, 1987).

The Camelot image of the Kennedy Administration was buttressed by two staunch loyalists, Theodore C. Sorensen and Arthur Schlesinger, Jr. Sorensen's *Kennedy* (New York, 1965) and Schlesinger's Pulitzer Prize winning *A Thousand Days: John F. Kennedy In The White House* (Boston, 1965) were brilliantly written and carefully argued. Other Administration figures soon contributed an assortment of valuable volumes. See Roger Hilsman, *To Move A Nation* (Garden City, New York, 1967), John Kenneth Galbraith, *Ambassador's Journal, A Personal Account Of The Kennedy Years* (Boston, 1969), W .W. Rostow, *The Diffusion Of Power: An Essay In Recent History* (New York, 1972), Maxwell Taylor, *Swords And Plowshares* (New York, 1972), Harris Wofford, *Of Kennedys And Kings* (New York, 1980), and Richard Goodwin, *Remembering America: A Voice From The Sixties* (Boston, 1988). See also Hugh Sidey, *John*

F. Kennedy, President (New York, 1963), a flattering account that had Presidential assistance.

The Kennedy Administration receives negative ratings in Victor Lasky, *J.F.K.: The Man And The Myth* (New York, 1963), Louise FitzSimons, *The Kennedy Doctrine* (New York, 1972), Henry Fairlie, *The Kennedy Promise: The Politics Of Expectation* (Garden City, New York, 1973), and Bruce Miroff, *Pragmatic Illusions: The Presidential Politics Of John F. Kennedy* (New York, 1976). See also Ralph G. Martin, *A Hero For Our Time, An Intimate Story Of The Kennedy Years* (New York, 1983). The most balanced and solidly documented history to date is Herbert S. Parmet, *JFK: The Presidency Of John F. Kennedy* (New York, 1983). See also J. Richard Snyder (ed.), *John F. Kennedy: Person, Policy, Presidency* (Wilmington, Delaware, 1988) and David Burner, *John F. Kennedy And A New Generation* (Glenview, Illinois, 1988).

On the Bay of Pigs fiasco, see Tad Szulc and Karl E. Meyer, *The Cuban Invasion* (New York, 1962), Haynes Johnson, *The Bay Of Pigs* (New York, 1964), Peter Weyden, *Bay Of Pigs* (New York, 1979), and Trumbull Higgins, *The Perfect Failure: Kennedy, Eisenhower, And The CIA At The Bay Of Pigs* (New York, 1987). For more on Administration and CIA machinations toward Cuba, see Thomas Powers, *The Man Who Kept The Secrets: Richard Helms And The CIA* (New York, 1979), Warren Hinckle and William W. Turner, *The Fish Is Red: The Story Of The Secret War Against Castro* (New York, 1981), and John Prados, *Presidents' Secret Wars: CIA And Pentagon Covert Operations Since World War II* (New York, 1986). Arthur M. Schlesinger Jr.'s *Robert Kennedy And His Times* (New York, 1978) contains a spirited defense of the Administration's Cuban policies.

The Berlin Crisis is discussed in Robert Slusser, *The Berlin Crisis Of 1961* (Baltimore, 1971), Jack M. Schick, *The Berlin Crisis, 1958–1962* (Philadelphia, 1971), and Curtis Cate, *The Ides Of August: The Berlin Wall Crisis Of 1961* (New York, 1978).

The Administration's approach to Southeast Asia may be studied in Neil Sheehan, et al., *The Pentagon Papers, As Published By The New York Times* (New York, 1971), David Halberstam, *The Best And The Brightest* (New York, 1972), Charles Stevenson, *The End Of Nowhere: American Policy Toward Laos Since 1954* (Boston, 1972), William J. Rust, *Kennedy In Vietnam* (New York, 1985), Ralph B. Smith, *An International History Of The Vietnam War: The Kennedy Strategy* (New York, 1986), and Ellen J. Hammer, *A Death In November: America In Vietnam, 1963* (New York, 1987).

On the Cuban Missile Crisis, see Elie Abel, *The Missile Crisis* (Philadelphia, 1966), Robert F. Kennedy, *Thirteen Days, A Memoir Of The Cuban Missile Crisis* (New York, 1969), Herbert Dinerstein, *The Making Of A Missile Crisis, October 1962* (Baltimore, 1970), Graham T. Allison, *Essence Of Decision: Explaining The Cuban Missile Crisis* (Boston, 1971), Abram Chayes, *The Cuban Missile Crisis* (New York, 1974), David Detzer, *The Brink* (New York, 1979), Lester Brune, *The Missile Crisis Of October 1962: A Review Of Issues And References* (Claremont, California, 1985); Raymond Garthoff, *Reflections On The Cuban Missile Crisis* (Washington, D.C.,

1987); Morris Morley, *Imperial State And Revolution: The United States And Cuba, 1952–1985* (New York, 1988); and James G. Blight and David A. Welch, *On The Brink: Americans And Soviets Reexamine The Cuban Missile Crisis* (New York, 1989). See also I. F. Stone, "What If Khrushchev Hadn't Backed Down?," in I. F. Stone, *In A Time Of Torment* (New York, 1968) and Barton J. Bernstein, "The Cuban Missile Crisis: Trading The Jupiters In Turkey?," *Political Science Quarterly*, 95 (Spring, 1980).

See George F. Kennan, *Memoirs, 1925–1950* (Boston, 1967), Charles Bohlen, *Witness To History, 1929–1969* (New York, 1973), Chester Bowles, *Promises To Keep: My Years In Public Life, 1941–1969* (New York, 1971), and Edward Crankshaw (ed.), *Khrushchev Remembers* (Boston, 1970). See also Edgar M. Bottome, *The Missile Gap* (Rutherford, New Jersey, 1961), Harvey S. Perloff, *Alliance For Progress: A Social Invention In The Making (1969), Richard B. Mahoney, JFK: Ordeal In Africa* (New York, 1983), Thomas J. Noer, *Cold War And Black Liberation: The U.S. And White Rule In Africa, 1948–1968* (Columbia, MO., 1985); William Attwood, *The Twilight Struggle: Tales Of The Cold War* (New York, 1987); Montague Kern, Patricia W. Levering, Ralph B. Levering, *The Kennedy Crises: The Press, The Presidency, And Foreign Policy* (Chapel Hill, 1983), Glenn T. Seaborg, *Kennedy And The Test-Ban Treaty* (Berkeley, 1983), and Bernard J. Firestone, *The Quest For Nuclear Stability: John F. Kennedy And The Soviet Union* (Westport, Conn., 1982). Useful biographies include Henry Trewhitt, *McNamara: His Ordeal At The Pentagon* (New York, 1971), Warren Cohen, *Dean Rusk* (Tatowa, New Jersey, 1980), and Thomas J. Schoenbaum, *Waging Peace and War: Dean Rusk In The Truman, Kennedy And Johnson Years* (New York, 1988). Richard J. Walton's *Cold War And Counterrevolution: The Foreign Policy Of John F. Kennedy* (Baltimore, 1972) is a left-wing attack.

On the Administration's approach toward civil rights, see Victor S. Nevasky, *Kennedy Justice* (New York, 1971), Carl Bauer, *John F. Kennedy And The Second Reconstruction* (New York, 1977), Wofford's *Of Kennedys And Kings*, Allen Matusow's *The Unraveling Of America: A History Of Liberalism In The 1960s* (New York, 1984), Stephen B. Oates, *Let The Trumpet Sound: The Life Of Martin Luther King, Jr.* (New York, 1982), and Taylor Branch, *Parting The Waters: America In The King Years, 1954–63* (New York, 1988). Other studies on domestic matters include Grant McConnell, *Steel And The Presidency, 1962* (New York, 1963), Seymour E. Harris, *Economics Of The Kennedy Years And A Look Ahead* (New York, 1964), Jim F. Heath, *John F. Kennedy And The Business Community* (Chicago, 1969), John M. Logsdon, *The Decision To Go To The Moon: Project Apollo And The National Interest* (Cambridge, Mass., 1970), and Gordon T. Rice, *The Bold Experiment: JFK's Peace Corps* (Notre Dame, 1986). See also Lewis Paper, *The Promise And The Performance: The Leadership Of John F. Kennedy And Social Welfare* (Lanham, Maryland, 1980), and David Burner and Thomas R. West, *The Torch Is Passed: The Kennedy Brothers And American Liberalism* (New York, 1984).

Miscellaneous works include Malcolm E. Smith, *Kennedy's 13 Great Mistakes In*

The White House (Smithtown, New York, 1968), Tom Wicker, *JFK And LBJ: The Influence Of Personality Upon Politics* (Baltimore, 1969), Theodore Sorensen, *The Kennedy Legacy* (New York, 1970), and Anthony Summers, *Goddess: The Secret Lives Of Marilyn Monroe* (New York, 1985), a study that discusses both John and Robert Kennedy and warrants careful attention.

The literature on the Kennedy assassination is vast. The place to begin is U.S. President's Commission On The Assassination Of President John F. Kennedy, *Report Of The Warren Commission On The Assassination Of President Kennedy* (New York, 1964). Other books requiring attention include Mark Lane, *Rush To Judgment* (New York, 1966), Anthony Summers, *Conspiracy* (New York, 1980), De Loyd J. Gurth and David R. Wrone, *The Assassination Of John F. Kennedy* (Westport, Conn., 1980), David S. Lifton, *Best Evidence: Deception And Disguise In The Assassination Of John F. Kennedy* (New York, 1981), Michael L. Kurtz, *Crime Of The Century: The Kennedy Assassination From A Historian's Perspective* (Knoxville, 1982), Jean Davison, *Oswald's Game* (New York, 1983), Henry Hurt, *Reasonable Doubt* (New York, 1985), and David W. Belin, *Final Disclosure: The Full Truth About The Assassination Of President Kennedy* (New York, 1988).

JFK can be read in U.S. Congress, *John Fitzgerald Kennedy: A Compilation Of Statements And Speeches Made During His Service In The United States Senate And House Of Representatives* (Washington, 1964) and President John F. Kennedy, *Public Papers Of The President Of The United States: John Fitzgerald Kennedy* (Washington, 1962, 1963, and 1964.) The Kennedy-Nixon debates of 1960 are in Sidney Kraus (ed.), *The Great Debates* (Bloomington, Indiana, 1962). See also Edwin O. Guthman and Jeffrey Shulman (eds.), *Robert Kennedy In His Own Words, The Unpublished Recollections Of The Kennedy Years* (New York, 1988). Books attributed to JFK include *Why England Slept* (New York, 1940), *Profiles In Courage* (New York, 1956), and *A Nation Of Immigrants* (New York, 1964). Scores of scholarly and popular articles were published in his name. For a bibliography of literature on Kennedy, see Joan Newcomb (ed.), *John F. Kennedy* (Metuchen, New Jersey, 1977). See also Thomas Brown, *JFK: History Of An Image* (Bloomington, Indiana, 1988).